WORLD WAR II DIARY

A Personal War Story
A Personal Love Story

By Martin and Vi Dusa

Compiled by Lee Dusa

Copyright © 2022 Martin and Vi Dusa. Compiled by Lee Dusa. *All rights reserved.*

ISBN 978-1-66785-283-6 (Print)

ISBN 978-1-66785-284-3 (eBook)

No part of this publication may be reproduced, distributed, or transmitted in any form or by any means, including photocopying, recording, or other electronic or mechanical methods, without the prior written permission of the authors, except in the case of brief quotations embodied in critical reviews and certain other noncommercial uses permitted by copyright law.

TABLE OF CONTENTS

Foreword 1

Martin and Vi – Their Beginnings 4

Transcription of Handwritten Diary (as it was written)
Published in a Book Prepared by Vi Dusa,
Wife of Martin Dusa, August 1994 17

Martin Dusa Letter to Son Lee 270

Martin and Vi – Life Together After the War 272

Addendum 277
    The China, Burma, India (CBI) Campaign – Priardoba Airfield 278
    About the Hellbirds 280
    Boeing B-29 Superfortress 282
    462nd Bombardment Group 284
    Major General Alfred F. Kalberer 285

FOREWORD

Our mother, Vi Dusa, created the Diary Book. On December 7, 1941 she sat, along with her then boyfriend, Martin Dusa and family members, huddled around the Motorola radio, as President Theodore Roosevelt exclaimed in his thunderous voice "this day shall live in infamy". The President, along with the whole US population was shocked by the bold Japanese attack on the US base at Pearl Harbor that day. Martin and Vi looked at each other with fear, knowing that their lives would be changed from that point forward. In fact, they were right. Their lives, and the lives of all Americans would be changed. The lives of just about everyone on the planet would be changed. Millions would be killed over the next four years. All because a few deranged country leaders were crazily motivated with an ambition to rule the world.

Vi and Martin knew war. Vi's father, Art Sessions, had returned only a few years earlier from the trenches of France where thousands had been killed in WWI. Vi was keenly aware of her father's military uniform still hanging in his closet. They were aware soldiers died in combat. They also knew that in war one country would win and one country would lose. On that day in December, 1941 they were mad at Hitler for earlier starting the war in Europe. Now they were mad as hell at Japan for starting the war in the Pacific which now directly involved the US. They knew they had to fight. Everyone had to fight to beat back this enemy who threatened their way of life. They would fight. They had to win. It was fear that drove their every decision from that day forward. Fear of losing, fear of dying.

This book is about that fear. But it is also about love. And it is about patriotism. And it is about history. And it is about two people dedicated, in their own way, to doing the right thing no matter the costs. This is a story about Vi and Martin.

That radio broadcast on December 7 set the wheels in motion for Vi and Martin. After having dated for two years they immediately decided to get married before Martin left. Their wedding was seven days later, December 14. For her part Vi decided to become the chronicler of events during the war, saving every written letter with her new husband, every newspaper clipping, every family photo. She felt that a record of their lives would be important for future generations to understand, especially if their lives together might be shortened if things did not go well in the war effort. She wanted to create a history of their time together. She did a remarkable job of preserving that history and later assembling those documents into this book.

Martin immediately knew that the events of that December day would change history forever. He knew this was a big deal in the evolution of mankind, even from his background of his little formal education. For his insight we all can be forever grateful for his effort in recording, in his own handwriting, his daily activities through four years of war. His fears, failings, successes, and wonderment as he traveled around the world on a mission to win is revealed poignantly. We learn a lot about the man, our father, through his experiences and his reaction to the horrors of war he observed. We not only learn about the activities of the war, but about his strong love for his new wife, and then two years later, his first son. His constant references to Vi revealed that this love was the strong attraction driving him to want to return home. That desire led him to doing the things he felt were the best decisions he could make to enable his return.

After traveling by troop ship across the Atlantic through the Suez to India, across India by train, and then again by ship around Australia he ended up on a small island in the Pacific called Tinian. It was from there the huge B-29's were launched in 1945. They were bombing the hell out of Japan in an attempt to end the war. He watched as 280 B-29's would take off en masse, four at a time on parallel runways at North Field, the largest airport in the world at the time, to make bombing runs to Japan. He knew many of the crews, some of those did not return. Martin watched as the atomic bomb was being loaded into the belly of the Enola Gay B 29. That very bomb, dropped on Hiroshima, Japan, would kill hundreds of thousands. It would end the war.

Finally, he came home to his love Vi, and his first son, me. I was born in 1943. I feel compelled to share the story of Mom and Dad as they are remarkable people for their love for each other. Their first four years together were marked by fear, by separation, and yet a strong hope and confidence that if they, and their fellow countrymen, did the right thing it might turn out alright someday. In that optimism they were right. Their lives turned out exceedingly well. They had four kids. I am the oldest, followed by Jerry, Jim and finally our sweet sister Maryann.

But I also see in Dad's diary an insight into the feelings of a man at war. A man who did not want to die yet believed strongly in the cause of the war. He wanted to win. He wanted the US to win. He was willing to work to make that happen. He was a patriot. After the war he was active in our local VFW chapter, proudly wearing his uniform as a member of the color guard at our local town parades every year. Mom was active in the women's VFW also, selling poppies every Memorial Day. America had won. They now turned their attention to raising their kids to hopefully have a better life than they had had. Hopefully a life without war. Without fear.

I have been intrigued by the question about why the US would send a large army of men and equipment to India during the war. Why was my father in Khagpoor, India? It had to do with China. Apparently, the US had decided to defend China from attacks from Japan in return for China letting the US set up an airbase in China from which they could reach Japan with bombers. (How things have changed between the US and China in just 80 years since 1942.) The only way to safely get to China at the time was to fly over the Himalayan mountains from India. Called "Over the Hump" it did not work out very well as Dad explains in his diary. Dad watched many heavily loaded airplanes explode or crash low on fuel in their long flights over the world's tallest mountains.

The big bombers used in the China campaign as well as the Pacific campaign were B-29's, the largest airplane in the world at the time. The US rushed them through design and construction at a torrid pace, believing they would be the punch necessary to bring Japan to their knees. They were right. Nearly 3200 B-29's were constructed and sent into service. As a brand-new airplane with new engines and new systems they were subject to failure. About 1200 were lost, along with their crews, due to mechanical failure. More were shot down in combat. But these huge beauties, as Dad called them, were impressive, and were instrumental in causing Japan to surrender.

My two brothers, along with our sister, are very close even today. Growing up with parents like ours we were taught the values of hard work, love for each other, and patriotism. We four feel that this book about Martin Dusa, along with his love, our mother Vi, needs to be shared with anyone who may appreciate a look into the very personal lives of a couple in time of war. We can thank our father for writing his diary, and our mother for assembling this book. We dedicate this work to their memory.

Lee Dusa
June 2022

MARTIN AND VI –
Their Beginnings

Mom was the oldest of three girls (Viola, "Vi", Margaret and Dorothy) raised by their parents Art and Mary Sessions in Alexandria, Minnesota. This was a decent, hardworking, church going family which could be described as "salt of the earth". Art built his own house on the shores of Lake Le Homme Dieu along old Hwy 29 a couple of miles north of Alex. The restaurant Zorbaz currently sits on that exact site. This whole area, now built up in houses, was originally the Sessions family farm; currently a street named Sessions Avenue bisects that land today. Art inherited the land from his father, John J. Sessions, who had acquired the acreage in the late 1800's. Located across Browns Point Road from the family home was a roller-skating rink/dance hall called the Gangplank. It was a center of social activity for people from miles around. The owners of that facility also sold sporting goods and bait and rented boats to visiting fishermen. Today the Gangplank is gone, and that location is occupied by a restaurant called Bugaboo Bay.

Arthur Sessions was industrious. He served in WWI in 1918 as an infantryman seeing action in the trench warfare in France. After returning from the war he operated his small farm, drilled water wells for customers with a rig he constructed himself, harvested blocks of ice in the winter from the lake and kept the ice stored under piles of sawdust in the old barn and sold it to resorts in the summer, built and operated a gas station along the highway in front of his home and added an ice cream concession called the Sugar Bowl which my Mom and her sisters manned during the summer. He was also a skilled carpenter and led the crew when our family home in Henning was built in 1947. He was a large, soft-spoken man with a kindly disposition. He taught his daughters the value of hard work, honesty in dealing with others, and perseverance as a means of survival. The family's hand to mouth existence was successful because it was driven by his devotion to earning income in any manner available. Mainly I remember him as a people person from my perspective as a two or three year old. I remember that he had a habit of "thumb twirling" as he sat in his easy chair after a hard day's work.

Mary Sessions, nee Schwartz, my grandmother, was short in stature and very hard working. She maintained a job each summer cleaning and cooking at a large private home around the lakeshore for a wealthy Texas family named Tennison. She was a no-nonsense kind of person who felt that one's worth was based on the amount of work they performed. She did not hold back comments when she felt something was being handled inappropriately. She was also very religious saying the rosary in her rocking chair at the end of every day. I got to know "Little Grandma" well as many years later I lived with her for two years in Sacramento while going to college.

Art and Mary supported their girl's education, even though they lived miles from Alexandria and the school. When the bus did not run, Art would take the girls into town in his car. Mom frequently had a late schedule because of her participation in the drum and bugle corps marching band. Playing in this band, which performed in parades and in band competitions was one of the highlights of Mom's early life. She loved parades and was riding on a float when Dad first spotted her from the crowd along the parade route. Parades would play an important part of their lives for many years.

Art and Mary had many relatives living nearby. Charlie and Nellie Payne had a home on the farm. Nellie was Art's sister. Nellie was a frail person, stayed home most of the time and kept a cage with birds in her enclosed porch. I remember the bad odor from that bird cage. Charlie was not held in high regard by other family members, but I don't remember why. Faye Sessions, another of Art's sisters, who never married, and one of my favorite people, also had a home on the farm. Faye was kind and helped Mom raise me for a time while Dad was gone during WWII. I remember playing in the wet sawdust in the ice barn behind Faye's house when I was very young. Mary's sister Tekla was married to Mr. August Fraisal and lived a few miles north on their farm. There were many Sessions and Schwartz cousins that lived on other farms in the area. One family, the Covels, did not live on a farm as Howard had a job in town working at the airplane factory. Their home was on the shores of Lake Carlos. They had two kids Jerry and Margaret who were near my age. On a few occasions during the fifties the whole gang of Mom's Alexandria based relatives would come to visit us in Henning, which is about an hour's drive north of Alex. There were so many of them that Jerry, Jim and I called them the baseball team (there are nine players per side times two teams makes eighteen on two clubs). It seemed like there were that many. Our little house could not accommodate that many people, so we frequently had picnics in our back yard.

During WWII the whole Sessions family moved to Sacramento, California for a couple of years. Dad had joined the service and was stationed at McClelland AFB in Sacramento in 1942. He won approval to live off base and asked his new wife (our mother) to join him there so she traveled to Sacramento, along with her father Art. Dad and Mom were married on December 14, 1941 one week after Pearl Harbor and he left for the service immediately thereafter. Art got a job folding parachutes at McClelland, so he asked his wife and the other two daughters Margaret and Dorothy to come to Sacramento also. It wasn't long before both girls met men, got married, and started their lives and families in Sacramento.

During the war, in late 1943, Dad was sent overseas so Mom (and me at a few months old) along with her folks Art and Mary left Sacramento and returned to their home in Alexandria, Minnesota. There I was tended to by Mom, her aunt Faye and my grandparents Art and Mary. In late 1945 Dad returned to Alex from the service and returned to his job at the Gamble Store in Alex.

The result of these moves was that the Sessions family was split between Alexandria, Minnesota (to include Henning, Minnesota) which included Art and Mary and Mom and Dad and Sacramento, California, which included Margaret and her husband Ted Bryte (and kids Mike and Carol), and Dorothy and her husband Claire Palmer (and kids Andy and Ken). When Art passed away in the fifties (heart attack) Little Grandma went to live in Sacramento to be close to her daughters Margaret and Dorothy. She lived alone in her own house at 1501 16th Avenue in the Oak Park area of Sacramento until she passed in the 1980's.

My Mom's family represented life in small town America, greatly influenced by two world wars, and a lifestyle reminiscent of the frontier of our countries' development. America had asserted itself during WWI and felt a national pride in that accomplishment. America went all out in their commitment to winning WW2 and that victory cemented this countries dominance as a world power. All Americans felt this hard-earned position in the world was well deserved and the resulting patriotism was demonstrated unabashedly at every opportunity. Mom and Dad were active in the VFW and the Women's VFW after the war. Each member of the Sessions family contributed to the war effort; Art packing chutes, Ted Bryte serving, Claire Palmer working on airplanes at McClelland, Dad in the 20th AF. Every family had a victory garden during the war, experienced gas, sugar, rubber and nylon rationing. After the war electric utilities kept pushing lines out to rural communities bring electricity to them for the first time through REA's (Rural Electrification Associations). The G I Bill of 1944 provided funding for education to returning vets and they took advantage of it. Education was viewed as the ticket to a better, happier lifestyle, less focused on basic survival which had driven their lives and more on the potential contribution the younger generation could make to a better America.

For her part, Mom provided support to her new husband (and the father of their son) by writing to Dad every day while he was gone during WW2. Her letters kept him going and he documented this in his diary. And she was disciplined in keeping the letters he sent to her, as well as the newspaper clippings of nearly every day reporting the news of the war. She considered these family treasures which she later turned into a WW2 family scrapbook called WW2 Diary which she published as a

187-page hard bound book for each of her four kids. Today that book is not only a family treasure but a national treasure as well as it documents in detail one man's contribution to the war effort.

Mom, because of her childhood environment in a resort community with visitors from large cities and faraway places, had an exposure to a more refined lifestyle than did Dad, because of the influence of the people visiting her neighborhood during the summers from larger cities. Her family lived in an area populated with many lakes which served as a destination for people from warmer states and larger cities who came there for recreation. Part time residents occupying their own cottages or temporary visitors in resort cabins increased the population significantly during the summer. Permanent residents made their living on small dairy farms or in service or business jobs in town. Summer was filled with the excitement of out of towners and visitors interested in fishing, relaxing, boating and socializing. Winter was duller as the summer surge was replaced by a normal life pattern with school activities the centerpiece for school age children. Small dairy farms populated the countryside and served as the primary economic base for the area.

She also, was one of three girls, all of whom were girly girls. They all came under the influence of their father, Art Sessions, who loved and treated them all well. They learned "class" from him as he practiced it in his own way. Her father's influence, along with her environment in the resort community, and a positive experience in school, caused Mom to be more refined and well behaved than Dad. She was the epitome of "Minnesota Nice".

After graduating from high school Mom attended an art institute in Minneapolis. She lived with her uncle and aunt in the city and rode the bus every day to class. She was studying to become a fashion artist, the person who draws fashions for newspaper and magazine ads. Returning home to Alex during the summer she worked at Anderson Furniture as a bookkeeper. It was during that time, in 1939 that she met Dad. That's when her life became a little wilder. She was riding on the Anderson Furniture Store float in the annual town parade seated in the queen's position, when Dad spotted her from the crowd and committed to himself at that moment that he was going to marry that girl. She was a real beauty and drew everyone's attention, especially young Martin Dusa.

Their courtship involved spending time with several other couples, going to area dances and movies. The Knights, Charlotte and Steven, and the Rueben Stenzels (he drove a Wonder Bread delivery truck) were among these friends. They reported that they all had a great time during these years. Dad was working in sales at Gambles and doing very well, earning the respect of the owners, and earning advancements on a regular basis. Then the war started for the US with the bombing of Pearl Harbor by the Japanese on December 7, 1941. Dad and Mom got married one week later, in Detroit Lakes, Minnesota on December 14, 1941 in a simple ceremony and he shipped out one month later.

Why they chose Detroit Lakes for the location for their wedding is a little bit of a mystery for me. One story is that Detroit is half way between his folks in Mahnomen and her folks in Alex so that travel would be equally divided between the two sets of parents. In fact, none of their parents attended. Another story is that, in looking for a venue, they could only schedule Detroit on short notice. It may be that (my conjecture) that they did not want to involve Mom's side of the family in their wedding. In any event, the oldest of the Sessions girls was now married. The newlyweds were unsure what would come next for them as the US dove headlong into a huge world war.

Dad's Side

Contrast the influence on us of Mom's family based on decency, refinement and education with our Dad's. Dad spent his early years growing up with his mother and father and three siblings in a tiny log cabin in a remote area of an Indian Reservation in northern Minnesota. It was near the Indian village called Naytahwash, population 75. Beside his siblings his only friends were Ojibway Indian children. The family's meager existence was totally reliant on fish and venison in addition to the vegetables they grew in their family garden. Family trips to the nearest town, Mahnomen, fifteen miles away, were infrequent. They worked hard on the acres Martin Dusa senior had acquired. His plan was to grow potatoes on land that they had to first reclaim from the thick forest.

With hand saws they felled the huge pine trees. Dad told stories from his childhood of the family dynamiting the stumps where teams of work horses pulled them to the side of the field where they were burned. Why did this family choose to be in that remote, unforgiving place? We have attempted to answer that question for the last 65 years with inquiries made to the remaining family members we can reach. With no concrete answers so far, we can only speculate.

It could be said that Dad was raised as "wild as an Indian". In many respects he was. Of course, it started with his father's journey to America.

Martin Dusa Senior, our grandfather, immigrated from a very small town (pop. 200) called Kalinova in (then) Hungary in 1905 at the age of 22. He was part of the second wave of Hungarian immigrants to the US. The first wave in 1895 was made up of professionals. The second wave, composed of working-class folks, was motivated to leave Europe after decades of little wars between countries as well as the lure of unlimited economic opportunity in America. In all, over two million Hungarians immigrated to the US between 1875 to 1915. The political instability in Europe was untenable and, in fact, led to the beginning of WWI in 1914 when Archduke Ferdinand was assassinated. Young Martin left Kalinova, traveled to Bremmer, Germany and boarded the passenger liner Barbarossa, never to return to Europe or home. Arriving in New York on Sept 21, 1905 and then working in the steel mills or coal mines of Pennsylvania for a few years, he sent money to his love,

Elizabeth to come join him in the US. She made the trip along with her sister Suzie. Martin and Elizabeth were married in Westmoreland, Pennsylvania May 31, 1909. The newly married couple moved to Wisconsin where their first child, Bill, was born. The threesome then moved to Iowa for a short time where he was probably employed on a farm. By September 12, 1918 at age 35 they had moved to Chicago where he owned and operated a saloon at 2103 Carroll Avenue. There both Dad and his sister Margaret (Muggs as she was affectionately called) were born. Dad recalled stories from his childhood of his mom, Elizabeth, lowering a basket on a rope to street vendors from their second floor home above the saloon to buy fruits and vegetables. After a few years in Chicago the Martin Dusa family sold the saloon in Chicago and moved to a log cabin in a remote part of the northern Minnesota woods onto an Indian reservation. The why of this move remains a mystery. We have tried to question family members, all of whom would not say, now they are gone. Documentation does not exist, as far as we now know. We keep trying.

Whether Martin owned the saloon or just operated it is unknown. Prohibition was gaining momentum making the long term economic prospects of the saloon business in Chicago a losing proposition. Martin must have felt this pressure. Started in the early 1800's the religious fundamentalists felt that alcohol was one of society's most important ills that had to be stamped out. Carrie Nation started a women's organization which invaded saloons with hatchets and broke up the booze bottles with axes. The Women's Christian Temperance Union would invade and occupy saloons and hold prayer services. States, like Kansas in 1881, started enacting anti-saloon laws prohibiting the sale of alcohol. Finally, in 1920, the US federal government adopted the 18 Amendment to the US Constitution making it illegal to sell or consume alcohol in the whole country. The booze business continued, although underground, via corruption of officials and through the ingenuity of the gangsters. Al Capone's future in Chicago was assured. Martin had to be looking for alternatives to this environment and he found one in northern Minnesota.

We family members are working to understand the push and pull of Martin and Elizabeth's decision to leave Chicago and settle in an extreme environment in northern Minnesota. It could be that the "push" was the effects of Prohibition on his Chicago saloon business. Maybe the mob had made contact with him in some way he felt was threatening?

White settlement of the rural land in Minnesota was driven by two major forces, the Homestead Act of 1862 and the emergence of the railroads in their push to the west. But first the Indian problem had to be solved. Of course, the Indians were there first, the Sioux in southern Minnesota and the Ojibway in northern Minnesota. They occupied the land and considered it theirs. The US government tried many times over many years to create an environment of peaceful co-existence by executing many treaties with the Indians. These contracts offered the Indians payments of money in return for allowing settlers to occupy land on the frontier in "Indian country". However, the Indians were continually squeezed into smaller and smaller parcels while the number of settlers increased, occupying more and more land. In the early part of 1860 the US government Indian agent from his office in Fort Snelling, Minnesota withheld monetary payment under some construed pretense. With that action the Indians had reached the end of their cooperation and staged a rebellion called the Minnesota Indian War of 1862. Over 800 white settlers were killed, hundreds of Indians died. The US Army was called in, even though the US Civil War was going hot and heavy, and the Indian rebellion was finally stopped. In 1864 in Fort Snelling three hundred and fifty eight Indian braves were jailed and about to be executed when President Lincoln stepped in and pardoned all but 38. Those 38 were hanged. The plan of allocating specific tracts of land called reservations gained momentum and the remaining Indians were forced by the government to locate within those reservations. There are several reservations throughout Minnesota today.

The Indian wars, with the heavy loss of life on both sides, took place in southern Minnesota involving the Sioux along with the Lakota and a few other tribes. Those tribes felt the pressure of hundreds of white settler families moving into lands they had lived on for centuries. The Ojibway in northern Minnesota were not treated any differently by the US government than the southern tribes but they did not openly rebel because there were fewer settlers in their territory. There were reasons that immigrants did not populate the north as much as the south. Northern Minnesota does not offer the same quality farming opportunities as southern Minnesota as the land is covered with thick forests, swamps and acidic soil. And the weather in northern Minnesota is more extreme. Northern Minnesota has a very short growing season and long, extremely cold winters.

The Ojibway (also known as the Chippewa) were placed in three reservations in northern Minnesota: the Red Lake, the Mille Lacs, and the White Earth. The Sioux were assigned other reservations in southern Minnesota. The Indians were promised, under these treaties, to be left alone to manage their own affairs on their respective reservations. However, the US government, under provisions in the Nelson Act of 1889, granted itself powers to sell the land to white settlers both inside the new reservations and on any lands previously occupied by Indians outside the reservations. The US government enacted these provisions driven by a desire to raise money to pay down the national debt, as well as to pave the way for white expansion of the west. These sales produced a revenue of $1.25 per acre for the government.

The Homestead Act of 1862 provided settlers 160 acres of land free of charge in return for an agreement to occupy and improve the land. The purpose of this Act, as expressed by the Congress of the US, was to populate the vast bare lands of the western US. It was intended that European immigrants would respond to this offer and many did. Over 1.4 million families took advantage of this offer; and groups from many countries of Europe established themselves in enclaves across mid America. It could be that the Martin Dusa family was one of these but I do not know for sure as of this writing whether he came to northern Minnesota under the Homestead Act or some other land offering. It has been reported that much of the desireable land suitable for farming was spoken for by 1900, and only marginal land was available when Martin decided to move out of Chicago. Martin and his family ended up in swamp type land with thick forests located about fifteen miles east of Mahnomen, Minnesota. This might have been an acquisition under the Homestead Act but I don't think so. At the time the Dusa family moved there the land had already been declared the White Earth Indian reservation. Martin might have heard about the Clapp Amendment to the Minnesota Constitution. Under that provision, passed in 1909, Indians living on the reservation could sell their land to non-Indians. Many did and today over 90% of the White Earth reservation is owned by non-Indians. Maybe Martin Dusa took advantage of this provision to acquire inexpensive land? Land ownership records on reservations are difficult, if not impossible to find as the reservations do not follow county or state procedures.

The greatest influence on westward expansion in Minnesota came at the hands of the railroads. The railroad barons of the day like James J. Hill had acquired millions of acres territorial land (read Indian) as a part of the agreement to build tracks to the far reaches of the frontiers of the west. The land granted to them was not only on which to build tracks, but to offer to settlers for a real cheap price as a way to populate the west. They knew that a railroad needed customers located in remote areas to order goods, and to transport their farm and forest products back to markets in the east, so the railroads became major players in the real estate business. They offered their lands for $1.25 per acre to anyone committing to move to these remote areas. In the late 1800's and early 1900's the railroads aggressively promoted the advantages of this low cost, productive land in newspaper ads, extensive brochures and traveling salesmen. They even sent representatives to European countries to promote the sales of these lands in mid America. The railroads told glowing stories of the freedom of individual land ownership and self-reliance which was appealing to many European families. The railroad provided a way to access these new lands out west; no longer were horse drawn wagons needed to travel long distances. The Northern Pacific was an early line running from Chicago thru northern Minnesota and on westward through North Dakota and points beyond. Perhaps young Martin in Hungary learned of this vast land full of opportunity? More than likely the Martin Dusa family used that railroad to travel to northern Minnesota from Chicago? Perhaps Martin purchased his land in Naytahwash from the railroad? Many settlers did but in Martin's situation I don't think so.

Economic activity in Minnesota was well under way when Martin and Elizabeth moved there from Chicago. Minneapolis had become a center for grain milling, contributing 15% of all flour to

sons were already farmed out to live with families in Mahnomen for schooling, he decided to move to town also. Upon moving to town Martin and Elizabeth built and operated a saloon at the corner of US 59 and SH 25, the busiest intersection in town. They called it the Road House. It is where the Shooting Star Casino stands today. Martin Sr. operated the Road House until he sold it when he became a city policeman.

In the early 1960's a new house was constructed for Ma and Pa in Mahnomen paid for by their four kids. It stands today on West Monroe Avenue. It was in this house that I remember a huge crock of poppy seeds grown by my grandmother in her large back yard garden stored in the porch. I would grab and eat a handful at a time.

To say that my grandfather led an exciting life is an understatement. Obviously, he kept trying to better his family's condition. Never did he become wealthy. He worked hard, valued family connections, and embraced change. While he and Elizabeth were married in a Catholic church and then remarried again 50 years later in a Catholic church in a ceremony in Mahnomen he was not a religious man. I remember him as fun loving, with jokes and stories and old-world songs in Bohemian sung at family get-togethers. They laughed a lot. He, along with his wife, loved life.

Dad moved into Mahnomen to continue his education. He lived with Mr. and Mrs. Neehassle in town in a very small house during his seventh and eighth grade school years. He got a job at a local Gamble Hardware store sweeping floors and dusting the displays. When the mechanical cream separator was invented Dad was enamored with this new technology and became an ardent promoter to visitors to the store. He rapidly gained a reputation for his sales success, was promoted to an outside sales position. He visited local dairy farmers and sold many units. By his late teens, he had purchased a car to support his sales efforts. When the motorized version of the old hand crank cream separator hit the market, and local farms installed electricity for the first time, Dad was quick to capitalize on the sales of this labor-saving tool for dairy farms. No longer did farmers have to spend hours with the hand crank of the old machine, separating raw milk into cream and milk. The owners of the Gambles Skogmo chain of hardware stores, headquartered in Fergus Falls, Minnesota noticed Dad's potential and promoted him to a more vibrant market in a larger city, Alexandria, located about 100 miles south. Dad move to Alex in about 1937 where he became an instant success in the Gambles store and soon became its top salesman. He was 21 years old. Charles Gamble became a huge supporter of Dad's blossoming career. Dad was adept at selling appliances for Gambles including washing machines, refrigerators, stoves and the like. "White goods" they were called. In one way or another he did this this rest of his life.

Dad's older brother Bill had met a girl in Mahnomen and married Hazel Walzwick from a local family. Bill and Hazel moved to Minneapolis after the war where Bill was employed as a plumber at

Jerry Baer Plumbing and Heating for his whole life. Dad's youngest sister Blanche married a local Mahnomen man by the name of Bennett Iverson who spent his working years as a janitor at the Mahnomen High School. Blanche was one of the top Avon sales reps in the US during her 50 year career with the company. Dad's other sister Margaret married Curtis Hurd who was a employee at a headquarters location of a large bank in St. Paul. Margaret sold real estate. Curt had a unique capability to accurately add a long list of numbers just by looking at them. Dad and his three siblings remained close until they all passed. They communicated frequently, visiting each other frequently and visited their folks they called Ma and Pa with frequent trips back to Mahnomen. This was a close family which demonstrated mutual respect for each other. These four "kids" had survived the log cabin/homestead adventure during their early lives and then all worked in their fathers Road House during that phase of their lives. Then the war started, with both Bill and Dad serving overseas, which in many ways affected all of them.

Our only cousins are Bob and Jeanne, children of Blanche and Bennett. Bill and Hazel did not have kids. Curt and Margaret adopted two brothers at one point (Henry and ?) but that did not work out well. Dad and Mom had the four of us, Martin Lee 1943, Jerry Arthur 1947, James William 1949, and Maryann Lizbeth 1955.

I think I was influenced with two different sets of inputs from each my father and mother as they each had come from different backgrounds as noted above. Mom represented to us a strong need for education, an artistic flair, and a solid homelife. She was thoughtful and creative. Always a rule follower, it was critical to her that one not only know the rules but adhere to them. In a more modified way, she interpreted the harshness of her mother's disdain for outlandishness in people's behavior as she led us in our upbringing. "Oh that's silly" little grandma would say. Mom practiced that but did not voice those particular words. Mom was the consummate peacemaker, not wanting to say outloud anything bad about anyone.

Dad, on the other hand was outgoing, energetic, goal oriented, enthusiastic, and hard working. He never stopped moving. He embraced change reflected by his quick acceptance of new technologies and frequent job changes. He believed in formal education to improve quality of life. He taught us to fish and hunt, both for the sport but primarily to feed the family. He modeled community service as an important contribution each of us is responsible for. He proved by his actions that leadership involved risk taking but was worth the results that could be obtained by stepping up when others might not. He was driven to provide for his family which he did to the best of his ability. For example, our family was treated to a higher quality of life compared to others due to his efforts (nice house in town, two cars, a duck hunting lease, a cabin at the lake, a new fishing/water ski boat, and college education for his kids). He was not driven by a quest for fame, power, or wealth. He felt these were beyond his reach due to his lack of a formal education as he left school after eight grade. He knew that education was the key to a better life and that is why he stressed that objective with each of us kids. In his own way, then, he provided very handsomely for his family. He did all this never making more than $8000. a year while they lived in Henning, a number obtained from his SS records. His practical approach worked. He was a strong, strong man. Both Mom and Dad made their contributions, each different, to our development.

Lee

TRANSCRIPTION OF HANDWRITTEN DIARY
(AS IT WAS WRITTEN)

Published in a Book Prepared by Vi Dusa,
Wife of Martin Dusa, August 1994

WAR II DIARY
BY MARTIN DUSA

W WAR II DIARY
BY
MARTIN DUSA

PRINTED AUGUST 1994, SACRAMENTO, CA
BY
VIOLA M. DUSA

DEDICATED
TO
OUR CHILDREN
AND GRANDCHILDREN
AND TO YOUR EXTENDED FAMILIES

This book is a true account which has been reproduced as written by your father and grandfather. It is my hope to create a continued interest in our family history.

With my love to all.

Mom

References
Personal Diary by Martin Dusa
Ex C.B.I. Round Up Magazine
Hellbird War Book
C.B.I. Theater of War Newspapers and Publications
The World Book Encyclopedia
Photo Collection by Martin Dusa
Scrapbook Items by Viola M. Dusa
Park Region Echo Newspaper, Alexandria, MN.

Pearl Harbor
December 7, 1941

The Beginning

THE JAPS' unexpected attack early on the morning of Dec. 7, 1941, caught us flatfooted and left this mass of wreckage and burned planes on Oahu.

The first and dirtiest battle went to the Japanese. On December 7th they killed our men in their beds, destroyed our planes on the ground. What was left didn't even add up to an air force and we had to rebuild before hitting the long and bloody road to Japan.

MOST OF OUR PLANES, like these P-40s, were shot up on ground.

JAPS' FIRST BLOW left Wheeler Field's hangars ravaged shambles.

WEDDING – DECEMBER 14, 1941

1311 IRVING ST.
ALEXANDRIA, MINNESOTA

OFFICIATE, FR. CANNON
DETROIT LAKES, MINNESOTA

Story of my army Life. Feb. 2, 1942

Yes, way back in Feb of 1942, one of the strangest things happened to me in my whole life I was reclassified into 1-A. So I went to work. I drove to Fargo N. Dak to Enlist in the Army in the Signal Corp. So they sent me to Fort Snelling, Minnesota for examination; I went there Feb 2, 1942. Stayed there until Feb. 5th, they then sent me home to get all personal things settled at home. Then on March 2nd 42, I left home one of the most sorrowed events of my life so at 5:30 I board a bus went to Fargo then at 11:30 that night a group of us got on a train to go to Fort Snelling. We got there the following morning. We marched about 12 blocks, then by truck to camp.

Story of My army Life. Feb. 2, 1942.
Yes way back in Feb of 1942, one of the strangest things happened to me in my whole life I was reclassified into 1-A. So I went to work. I drove to Fargo N. Dak. to Enlist in the army in the Signal corp. So they sent me to Fort Snelling Minnesota for examanation I went there Feb. 2 1942. Stayed there until Feb, 5 the then they sent me Home to get all personal things settled at home then on March 2nd 42, I left home one of the most sorrowed events in my life. Lo at 5:30, I Board a Buss went to Fargo. then at 11:30 that night a group of us got on a train to go to Fort Snelling we got there the following morning we Marched about 12 blocks then by truck

---

REGISTRATION CERTIFICATE 304
This is to certify that in accordance with the Selective Service Proclamation of the President of the United States

Martin Dusa
(First name) (Middle name) (Last name)
ALEXANDRIA, DOUGLAS, MINNESOTA
(No. and street or R. F. D. No.; city or town, county and State)
has been duly registered this 18 day of October 1940

Etta Albjornsen
(Signature of registrar)

Registrar for ONE ALEX MN.
(Precinct) (Ward) (City or county) (State)

BE ALERT — Keep in touch with your Local Board.
Notify Local Board immediately of change of address.
CARRY THIS CARD WITH YOU AT ALL TIMES
D. S. S. Form 2

Martin Dusa (signature)

NOTICE OF CLASSIFICATION

Local Board No. 1 — 74
Douglas County — 041
DEC. 16, 1941 — 001
Alexandria, Minnesota

Board of Appeal, by vote of ___ to ___
Class 1-B (Until _____, 19__).

Date of mailing DEC. 16, 1941
NOTE: RIGHT TO APPEAL

D. S. S. Form 57
(Rev. 5-20-41)

NOTICE OF CLASSIFICATION

Registrant: MARTIN DUSA JR.
Order No. _____
has been classified by—

LOCAL BOARD No. 1 — 74
DOUGLAS CO. — 041
DEC. 31, 1941 — 001
ALEXANDRIA, MINNESOTA

Local Board ☐ Board of Appeal, by vote of ___ to ___ ☐
President ☐ In class **1-A** (Until _____, 19__).

Date of mailing _____, 19__
Member of Local Board.

BE ALERT
The laws requires you—
To keep in touch with the local board.
To notify it of any change of address.
To notify it of any fact which might change classification.

NOTE: RIGHT TO APPEAL
Appeal from classification by local board or board of appeal must be made at office of local board, by signing appeal

★ ★ ★
★ ★ ★
★ ★ ★

MARTIN DUSA
LEE STENHJEN
BERT THOMPSON
MARK MAURIN
AL CARLSON
MINEHART BRUTLAG
BUD BAUER
ARNDT MYRVOLD
SIDNEY BACCHUS

Gamble Stores

23 Go To Snelling For Examination

Twenty-three men left at 6:55 o'clock Tuesday evening for a pre-induction examination at Ft. Snelling. They were treated to a 75c steak dinner at the Alexandria Cafe by the draft board before embarking. Those who pass will return for 30 days to settle any matters they wish before being inducted.

Of the twenty-four men originally scheduled to leave, only one was delayed. He was Victor Ringdahl who is under quarantine because of scarlet fever.

Those who left are: John Juberian and John Chase, Osakis; Helmer Magnuson, Parkers Prairie; Francis Haabla, Arnold Josephson, Arnold Ellingson, Joseph Thompson, Kensington; Orie T. Peaslie, Carlos; Carlyle Johnson, Moorhead; Alfred Garvin, Irvin Knapp, Arthur Linden Johnson, Martin Dusa, Jr., Odell Sannes, Lawrence Stoetzel, Lawrence Stahl, Kenneth Lang, Bert Skramstad and James Mehl, Jr., Alexandria; Lyle Gulbranson, Farwell; Nick Adensam, Carlos; Raymond Eastlund, Nelson; Earl Albertson, Garfield.

Martin Dusa, who has been employed as a traveling salesman by the Gamble Store the past three years, enlisted in the U. S. Signal corps and will leave for the army the first week of March.

He originally came from Mahnomen, where he was employed by the Gamble store for two years. Mrs. Dusa, employed as a cashier at the new National Tea store, will remain here.

Dusa said he is happy to serve his country, but is sorry to leave the many friends he made here.

CARD OF THANKS

Inasmuch as I am leaving for the army on March 3, I would like to thank all my customers for their business, while I was employed at the Gamble Store, and I wish to say goodbye to all my friends.

Martin Dusa.

In Honor of Martin Dusa who left for the army Monday evening a party was given at the Tolena Club by twenty-four of his friends.

GAMBLE STORES, ALEXANDRIA, MINNESOTA
STANDING, AL CARLSON, LES NORGARD, MGR.
LES HOLMES-RADIO-T.V., JOE AXELSON,
FRONT ROW, BILL VANDERCOOK, MARTIN DUSA

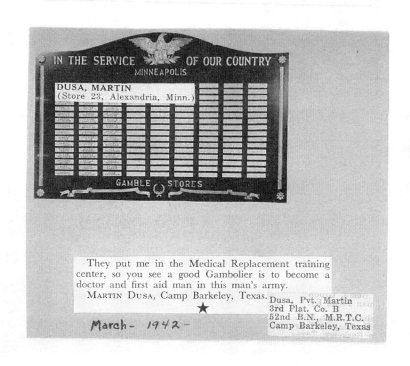

They put me in the Medical Replacement training center, so you see a good Gambolier is to become a doctor and first aid man in this man's army.
MARTIN DUSA, Camp Barkeley, Texas.

Dusa, Pvt. Martin
3rd Plat. Co. B
52nd B.N., M.R.T.C.
Camp Barkeley, Texas

March - 1942 -

ALEXANDRIA INSURANCE AGENCY
GEORGE & ORIES' INSURANCE BUILDING   PHONE 376-M
ALEXANDRIA, MINNESOTA

February 16, 1942

To Whom it May Concern:

I have known Martin Dusa for some time and I do not hesitate to write this letter to confirm his ability as a radio expert. Not only is he qualified in radio, but he has considerable ability along mechanical lines.

He is energetic and a willing worker, always pleasant and ambitious. If there is anything to be done, he'll do it.

Very truly yours,

Orie D. Olson

ODO:M

Also recommended by the following persons:

F. M. Uznnok, Secretary of Board of Public Works.
R. E. Schwark - Supervisor for Gamble Stores
L. R. Norgard, Manager Gamble Stores
Elow Hanson, Chief of Police
Alderman J. E. Kissner, Alexandria Minn.
Theodore Osding - Instructor - Alex. Public Schools
C. Fred Hanson, County Atty.
R. W. Putnam, President Farmers Nat Bank Alexandria
G. M. Olsen, Mgr. J.C. Penney Co.

So we were processed, examined again, and Sworn in the army. We had an IQ test, aptitude test; mine was 117, 112 so they classified me and put me in the Medical Corp. We were waiting for shipment. Rumors ran fast where we might go. Everyone had a different idea when and where. So we stayed there just one week. I called my wife each evening. Also sent home my civilian suit and bought a few things I needed. So on Sat March 9th I put in for a 24 hr pass to go to St. Paul to visit my Sister so on Sat night I called Vi to come to St. Paul from Alexandria, so she came by bus and Sunday morning at 8 AM to Camp so we were processed examined again and sworen in the army we had our IQ test apptitude, Mine was 117, 112, so they classified me and put me in the Medical Corp, we were waiting for shippment Romers ran fast where we might go every one had a diffrent Idea when & where. so we stayed there just one week. I called up my Wife each Evening and also sent home my civilian suit and Baught a few things I needed so on Sat March 8th I put in for a 24 hr pass to go to St Paul to visit my Sister so on Sat night I called Vi to come to St Paul from Alexandria, so she came by Bus and Sunday Morning at 8 A

RECEPTION CENTER
Fort Snelling, Minnesota

ORGANIZATION Receiving Co. # 2   Mar. 8, 1942   194_

Pvt. Dusa, Martin (NMI)   17049855   Rec. Co. # 2 Ft. Snelling, Minn.
(Grade, Name, Serial Number and Organization)
has permission to be absent from his organization and station
from: Mar. 8, 1942 10:30 A.M. to: Mar. 9, 1942 6:30 A.M.
for the purpose of visiting Wife St. Paul, Minn.

V Yelkin - 2nd Lt Inf
VIRGIL V. YELKIN
2nd Lt. Inf.
~~Commanding~~

/crc

Dusa

I get my pass Low and Behold I met my wife and Sis and we went to Church and then had a Big dinner at the house where Muggs stayed then we went to town later we went to a show. So we went to Vi's uncle Joe's and had Supper stayed there until 1:30 AM Vi got a bus and went to Alex, sure was a sad moment. So Joe took me to camp Monday the next day. We got all our stuff packed and put in separate groups for different camps. So at 6:30 PM we boarded a troop train headed for Abiline, Texas We got there March 12, we were assigned Barracks 52BN Co. A 3rd plat. M.R.T.C. Camp Barkley, Texas. We were issued some clothes and put on a pay roster at $21.00 a month. No allotment.

I got my pass Low & Behold I met my Wife & Sis we went to Church then had a Big Dinner at the House where Meggs stayed, then we went to town later we went to Lowlow. So we went to Vi's uncle Joe's and had Supper stayed there until 1:30 A.M. Vi got a Bus & went to alex, sure was a sad moment. So Joe took me to Camp. Monday the next day we got all our stuff packed and put in separate groups for diffrent Camps so at 6:30 PM we Boarded a troop train headed for abline, texas we got there March, 12, we were assined Barrapes 52 BN. Co. A. 3rd Plat. M.R.T.C Camp Barkly Tfas we were Isued some clothes put on a pay roster at $21:00 a month. no allotment

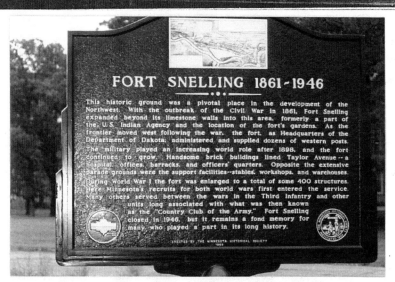

MINNEAPOLIS, MINNESOTA
INDUCTION CENTER

Saying 'GOODBYE' to my Wife, VI

SUNDAY
MARCH 9, 1942
ST. PAUL, MN.
MARTIN AND
MARGARET
DUSA - SISTER

We bought our stamps, the deduction of $6.90 for $1000. Insurance policy – it was compulsory to take out; at least $1.25 per month so that left me with $12.85 for a month. Well Texas sure was the place. Basic Training up at 4:30 AM, drilled, school, bivouac, obstacle course and physical training; almost drove me crazy. Vi wrote each day and sent me packages; over 9 weeks of training were almost over. Each Eve from 6 oclock until 9 PM I went to NCO school. Studied most everything; office work, little in general about the Army. So on May 9th we were to break up. Some were sent over seas, some to other camps. I with 34 others boarded a train at 5:30 Tues to leave for California. Some got off in

we Baught our own stamps, the Deduction 6.⁹⁰ for $1000.⁰⁰ Insurance policy, it was Conpulsery to tape out at least $1.25 Bond per month. So that left me 12.⁸⁵ for a month, Well Texas sure was the place Basic training up at $4.³⁰ AM drilled, School Bivouac and opstical coruse, phisical training almost drove me crazy, Vi wrote Each day sent me packages, our 9 weeks of Training were almost over. Each Eve from 6.oclok until 9PM I went to N.C.O. School studied most every thing office work. little in Genral about the army. So on May 9th we were to Brake up. some were sent over seas, some to outher Camps I with 34 outhers Boarded a train at 5.³⁰ true to leave for California some got off in

CAMP BARKELEY, TEXAS

52 51st Medical Training Battalion
Camp Barkeley, Texas

BASIC TRAINING MARCH 1942

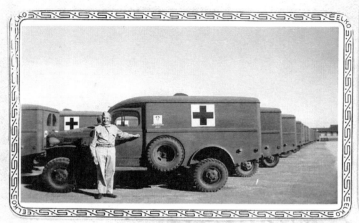
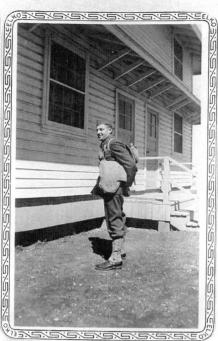

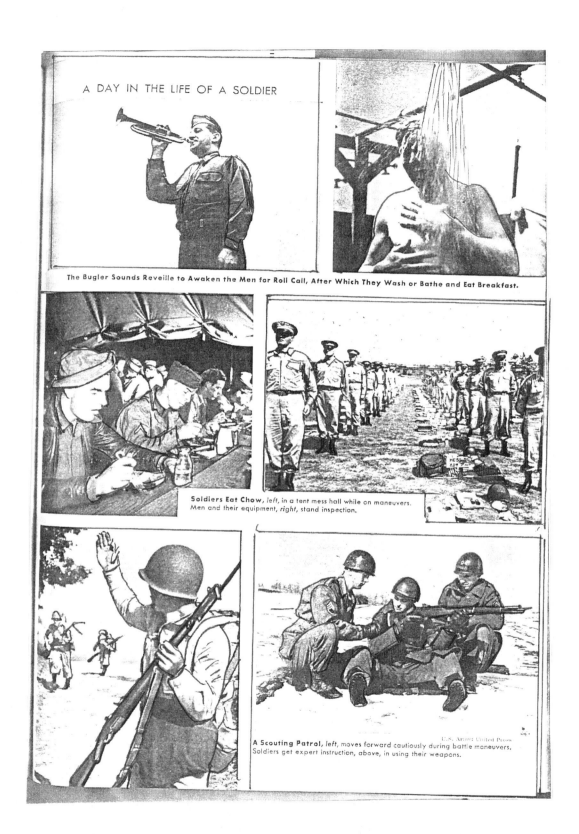

Arizona, some in L. A. and I went to Sacramento to McClellan Field. We lived in tents, some were assigned to the Station Hospital. I, with a few others, were assigned to the 23rd Air Depot Group to leave for Calcultta, India. Fortune or faith came when I got friendly with a Captain Hill. Very nice man. I told him I could cook or butcher, so he got me a transfer out of the Medical Corp. Eugene V. Hardy was the First Sgt of the 10th Station Compliment. He didn't like the way I got my transfer, so he had a dislike for me. Capt. Hill said I was in the permanent part and I could get my wife to come and stay with me.

Arizona some in L.A. and I went to Sacramento to McClellan Field we lived in tents some were assined to the Station Hospital, I with a few authers were asined to the 23rd air Depot Group to leave for Calcutta India, Your turn or waits come when I got Freindly with a Capt. Hill. Very nice man, I told him I could cook or Butcher, so he got me a Transfer out of the medical corp Ugine V. Hardy was the First Sgt of the 10th Station Complent he dident like the way I got my trensfer so he had a dislike in me. Capt Hill said I was in the permant part and I could get my Wife to come & stay with me.

JOHN V. COLLUCCI

ABOVE TENT CITY McCLELLAN A.F.B. SACRAMENT

Wm. Shakespeare, GOOD FRIEND

Is authorized to ration with the 10th Station Complement Mess.

Commanding Officer

McCLELLAN FIELD, CALIFORNIA

DEBIT
CREDIT

DATE 5-15-43
1:15 P.M.

STATION: McClellan Field, California
ISSUING ORGANIZATION: POST CASUAL DETACHMENT

ISSUED TO) Martin Dusa. Pvt. 17049855
TURNED IN BY)

QUANTITY	UNIT	ARTICLE
1	ea	Cot, folding canvas
1	ea	Mattress
1	ea	Pillow
1	ea	Cover, Mattress
3	ea	Blanket, Wool O.D. 3 1/2#
1	ea	Pillowcase
2	ea	Sheets
1	ea	R.C. No. 1993

I acknowledge receipt of above listed (Quartermaster - Ordnance - Squadron - Air Corps - Signal Corps) Property.

Martin Dusa
55-nd M.R.T.C. Camp Barkely
Texas

DELIVER TO | Date 1/25/43

Attention ..... Cpl. Martin Dusa,
Coordination ..... Station Complement,
Immediate Action ..... POST.
Signature
Comment
Information
Preparation of Reply
Necessary Action
Compliance
Note and File
Note and Return
Information for Reply

This is furnished you for your own private use with the compliments of the Public Relations Officer.

Richard I. Nimmons
RICHARD I. NIMMONS,
Captain, Air Corps,
Public Relations Officer

Fold Here for Return

FROM
TO   Inter-Office Mailing Slip

PERMISSION GRANTED
TO LIVE OFF POST.

He would give me permission to live off the post. So on June 17th I went and rented a one room apartment at Ballentines for $4.00 a week. I wired for Vi to come. So on June 22nd Vi came at 4:45 AM. Oh I was happy to see her so we enjoyed the visit, saw a few sights. Each day I would get a pass to come home so on July 1st Vi and I set out to look for a job. She went to work at the Telephone Co. 17.00 a week. She worked there until the 17th of July and quit to work at the Spreckels Sugar Co $120.00 a month. Things were going well and we were very happy. I worked as a butcher. Then on July 1st I made PFC. Then on July 22nd Bud and Margaret, my Father in Law and Sister in Law drove my car, a 1939 Ford Coupe.

He would give me permission to live off the post. so on June 17th I went and rented a one Room apartment at Ballentines for 4⁰⁰ a week so I Wired for Vi to come he' on June 22ⁿᵈ Vi came at 4:45 A.M. oh I was Happy to see her so we Enjoyed the Visit saw a few sights, Each day I would get a pass to come Home to an July 1st Vi & I set out to look for a Job. she went to work at the Telephone Co. 17⁰⁰ a week she worked there until 17th of July & quite to go to work at Sprecks Sugar Co. $20⁰⁰ a month, things were going well we were Very Happy I worked as a Butcher. then on July 1st I made P.F.C. then on July 22ⁿᵈ Bud & Margeret My Father in Law & Sister in Law. drove My car 1939 Ford Coupe

9 & 12 lbs. STRIPPED BASS
SAN JOAQUIN RIVER
DOCTOR DONALD YEE
FISHING PARTNER

REC'D
P.F.C. RATING
JULY 1, 1942

1939 FORD COUPE

They arrived the 27th of July, no trouble what so ever. They lived with us at Ballentines. I took Bud and Muggs to the Field and they both got a job at the Field, she as a typist and he as a (parachute) packer. I used my car to travel back and forth to camp and always had a fresh supply of meat and food. Then on 27th of August Mary and Dot came. (my Mother in Law and another Sister in Law). We rented a house at 1348 58th Street Sacramento. We all lived together, bought furniture, fixed a garden, had it nice. But need I say now the idea of living together gets tiresome so on 19th of November I rented a beautiful 5 room for $35.00 a month at 1615 ½ 16th Street. Gee we sure had a wonderful time. Then on October 15 I made Corporal. Then on Jan 28 I made Sgt.

arrived the 27th of July no trouble what so ever. they lived with us at Balentines, I took Bob & Muggs to the field & they both got a job at the field she as a typist & Bob as a packer. I used my car to travel back & forth to camp and always had a fresh supply of meat & food then on 27th of ~~october~~ august. Mary & Dot come. we rented a house at 1348-58 st. Sacramento we all lived together Bought furniture fixed Garden had it nice. But need I say more the Idea of living together gets tiresome so on 19th of nov. I rented a Beautiful 5 rooms for $35.00 at 1615½-16th st. Gee we sure had a wonderful time then on october 15 I made corporal. then on Jan 28 I made Sgt.

1615 ½ 16TH ST.

REC'D SERGEANT RATING – JAN. 28, 1943

1348 58TH ST. SACTO, CA

ARTHUR AND MARY SESSIONS
MARGARET AND DOROTHY
VIOLA SESSIONS DUSA

friends at....
McCLELLAN FIELD

Rudi pd
Rollins pd
Butcher pd
Valentine pd
Thorson pd
Prince pd

Kelley pd
Stahl pd
Blades pd
Berg pd

Office Phone	Name, Rank & Organization	Address	Name Phone
402	Ballantyne, W.P., T/Sgt., M.C.	Post McClellan SACRAMENTO	514
	Holmes, T. C., M/Sgt., A.C.	Collitti	

Friday, December 25, 1942

–1942 Christmas

TO AIR DEPOT NEWS, McCLELLAN FIELD, CALIFORNIA

At McClellan–

10th STATION COMPLEMENT MESS

WM. SHAKESPEARE
1st Lt. Air Corps
MESS OFFICER

PATRICK J. COYNE
2nd Lt. Air Corps
Ass't Mess Officer

S/Sgt. C. H. SMITH
Mess Sergeant

S/Sgt. W. J. McGILL
S/Sgt. WAYNE NELSON
S/Sgt. G. A. VALENTINE
Sgt. O. T. TWEETEN
Cpl. EMANUEL ROLLINS
Assistants

Mr. JOHN W. BASICH
Bookkeeper

MENU
ASSORTED FRUIT COCKTAIL
HEARTS OF CELERY
STUFFED OLIVES
ICEBERG LETTUCE
RUSSIAN DRESSING
ROAST YOUNG WESTERN
TOM TURKEY
NEW ENGLAND OYSTER DRESSING
CANDIED YAMS   CRANBERRY SAUCE
IDAHO POTATOES A LA WHIP
GIBLET GRAVY COMMODORE STYLE
SELECTED IOWA CREAMED CORN   BUTTERED SIFTED PEAS
BREAD   BUTTER
PUMPKIN PIE   SOUTHERN FRUIT CAKE   MINCE PIE
AMERICAN CHEESE   SWISS CHEESE
ASSORTED CHRISTMAS CANDIES
GRAPES   ORANGES   APPLES
CIGARETTES
MIXED NUTS

In June of 1942 the government passed the increase in pay of soldiers to $50.00 a month, then the allotment bill passed for the wife. That gave us a good start. Then on the 23rd of Dec. I bought Vi a Russian Squirrel Look fur coat and hat for $200. She was very happy to get it. Then in Feb we discovered we were to have a blessed event in our family. We were so happy to hear this news. On October 15th I got a Furlough. I went by train to Minnesota to see the Folks. I was anxious to get back. Then on May 21, 1943, Vi was very sick. I took her to the hospital for an examination. She had a kidney infection. So I took her to Dr. Hale, a kidney specialist. He cured her and that all helped us.

in June of 1942 the Government passed the increase pay of soldiers to $50.00 a month then the allotment bill passed. for the Wife that gave us a good start then on the 23rd of Dec. I Bought Vi a Russian Squrell Jack fur coat & Hat for $200.00 she was very Happy to get it. then in Feb, we discovered we were to have a Blessed Event in our family we were so Happy to hear this news. in october 15th I got a Furlough I went by train to Minnesota see the Folks. I was anxious to get back. then on May 21, 1943 Vi was very sick I took her to the Hospital for a examination she had a Kidney Infection so then I took her to Dr. Hale a Kidney speciolest he cured her and that Dr. helped us.

CHRISTMAS 1942
IN
SACRAMENTO, CA

I still worked as a butcher, the work piled up. Things were getting tough at McClelland Field. So on July 26th an order came through for 10 men to be shipped to Camp Ripley, Minnesota. My name wasn't on the order. But I found out it would be possible for me to go. So I struck out a Chinese boys name (Shun Lee) and put my name on top. Vi gave me permission to go. So I got the car all fixed up and moved the things out of the apartment and packed a lot of things to take home. So on the 31st of July we got paid and picked up all the records. The car packed and at 9:30 AM July 1st 43 Ralph Ravelli and I drove to the Field

I still worked ccs the worked piled up. getting tough a so on July 26th for 10 men to be s Ripley Minnesota My the order. But I f be possiable for me out a Chinese Boys and put my own on permission to go. fixed up and moved the apartment and things to take home July we got paid & the car packed and Ralph Rovelli & I drove

a Butcher the things were McClellan Field a order come through hipped to camp name wasent on found out it would to go. So I struck name Shun Lee. top Vi gave me the so I got the car all the things out of packed a lot of so on the 31st of fixed up all records at 9:30 AM July 1st 43 to the Field

TRANSFERRED INTO 1280 M.P. CO. (AVN)

LITTLE FALLS MINNESOTA

RALPH AND MARTIN

and said So Long to all the friends. And at 11:30 we started on our trip for Minnesota. The first stop was Rock Springs, Wyo. Then Rock Island, Neb. Then Alexandria Minnesota. The trip was made without trouble, it was 2038 miles, we made it in 44 hours, we were glad the trip was over. We went to Mahnomen to my folks. We stayed there a few days, then on the 9th we reported to the Camp. We formed the 1280th MP Co (AVN). I was classified as a cook. Capt Bell was our C. O. I made the biggest mistake of my life. I volunteered to leave my wife to go to the first M. P. T. C. We trained there until

said solong to all friend and at 1130 we started on our trip for Minnesota the first stop was Rock Springs Wyo. then Rock Island Neb. then alexandria Minnesota the trip was made without trouble it was 2038 miles we made it in 44 hrs we were glad the trip was over. we went to mahnomen to my folks we stayed there a few days then on the 9th of aug we reported to the camp. we formed the 1290th M.P.co (AVN) I was classified as a cook capt Bell was our C.O. I made the Biggest mistake of my Life I Volunteered to Leave my Wife to go to the first 1st M.P.T.C. we trained there until

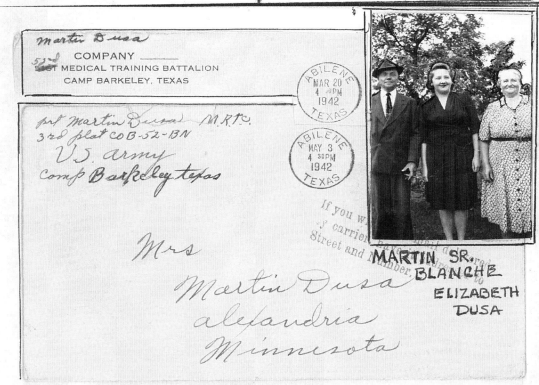

MARTIN SR.
BLANCHE
ELIZABETH
DUSA

the 25th of Sept. All the time at Ripley I went home often and awaited the news of the birth of our child. Behold on the 23rd of Sept 1943 the good news came; a baby boy weighed 9 ½ pounds and all is well. That really was a load off my mind to know that she and baby are well. Then we packed up everything to leave for Camp Barkley. Texas. I thought I could drive down there but I couldn't get permission so I sold my car for $700. cash and bought bonds. I put the bonds in a box at the Farmers National Bank, Alexandria Minnesota. Then we went back (oh yes, that was Sept 14, 1943). So we left Ripley the 25th of Sept. all the time at Ripley I went home after and awaited the news of the birth of our child. Behold on the 23rd of Sept 1943 the Good news came a Baby Boy weight 9½ Lbs and all is well that really was a load of my mind to know that she & Baby are well. Then we packed up every thing to leave for Camp Barkeley Texas. I thought I could drive down there But I couldn't get permission So I sold my car for $700.00 cash & Bought Bonds I put them in a Box at the Farmers National Bank Alexandria Minn. Then went back (Oh yes that was Sept 14, 1943.) So we left Ripley

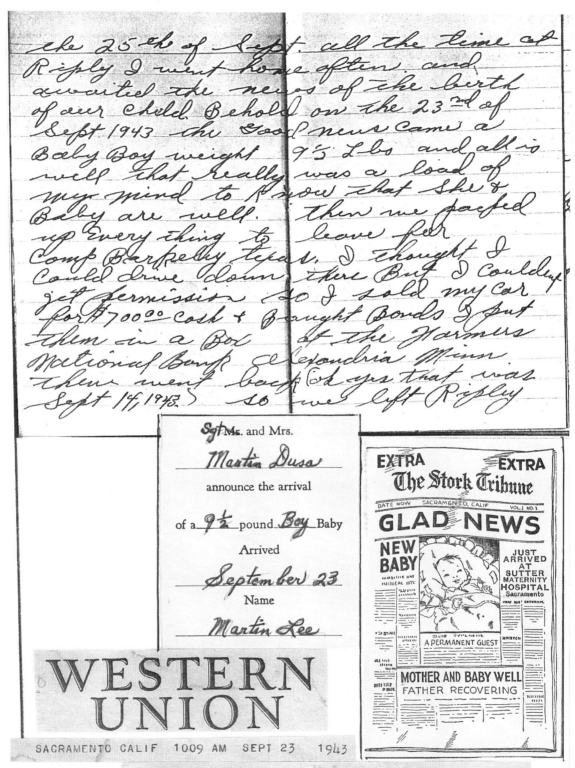

Sgt. ~~Mr.~~ and Mrs. Martin Dusa announce the arrival of a 9½ pound Boy Baby Arrived September 23 Name Martin Lee

WESTERN UNION

SACRAMENTO CALIF 1009 AM SEPT 23 1943

BOY BORN 600 AM WEIGHT 9 1/2 POUNDS BOTH FINE LOVE

The Stork Tribune — EXTRA EXTRA — SACRAMENTO, CALIF — GLAD NEWS — NEW BABY — JUST ARRIVED AT SUTTER MATERNITY HOSPITAL Sacramento — A PERMANENT GUEST — MOTHER AND BABY WELL FATHER RECOVERING

MP Training Units Moved To Barkeley

Movement of the First Military Police Training center (aviation), an Army Air force unit, from Camp Ripley, Minn., to Camp Barkeley, has been completed, it was announced Saturday at headquarters of Lt. Col. Ernest G. Buhrmaster, the commanding officer.

Since it was activated last June the unit had been in training at Camp Ripley, which has been abandoned by the Army — at least for the winter months.

Mission of the MP center at Barkeley is to train military police companies, (aviation) for overseas or domestic duty. In turn, missions of these companies will be to safeguard Army Air force installations throughout the world.

In addition to training of these companies, plans also call for activation of an officer candidate school and an officers' refresher course, both of these at an early date.

The MP Center will handle activation of new companies, reception of recruits, placement, training and shipment of companies to stations of duty. At present companies are given basic training of 10 weeks' duration. This includes field training plus specialization in various phases of military police duty.

Indications are that the center will be a permanent installation at Barkeley. It will have facilities for training and housing some 10,000 officers and enlisted men.

OVERSEAS VET AT HELM

Headquarters of the new unit is in the building that served as last headquarters of the 45th division at Barkeley, but since used by various units, last of these being the 30th Medical regiment.

Colonel Buhrmaster, commander of the MP center, has seen overseas service in the current war. He was assistant provost marshal in London and served as provost marshal in the 12th Air force, commanded by Gen. Jimmie Doolittle, during the invasion and occupation of North Africa. He was returned to the United States to activate the unit he now commands.

The MP Center is under control of the Air Service command, Patterson Field, O., and the air provost marshal, Washington, D. C. Executive officer of the Center

See MP CENTER, Pg. 6, Col. 7

So you see Sweet we don't know where we might be sent I hope we are Lucky (XXXXXXXX)

Sunday Morning, October 3, 1943

MP CENTER--
(Continued From Page One)

is Maj. Martin E. Davy, Syracuse, N. Y. Major Davy was given this assignment in July, and prior to that was executive officer of the 518th MP battalion of the First Army, commanded by Lt. Gen. Hugh A. Drum. On active duty since April, 1941, Major Davy prior to that was with the U. S. Department of Justice in the state of Washington.

Other key officers of the center are Maj. Paul Hitler, adjutant; Maj. Harold R. Noack, director of schools and training; Capt. Carlton M. Arthur, operations and training officer, and Capt. Edgar R. S. Steele, supply and transportation officer.

Schools operated by the center include judo, chemical warfare, first aid, sanitation, motor vehicle and motorcycle drivers, criminal investigation, weapons, and cooks and bakers school.

Traffic control and town patrol training is part of the general training program given all members of the MP companies.

Already active at Barkeley is the 394th AAF band under the direction of W. O. William O. Bowers. The band is the official musical unit of the center.

Europe's most active volcanos, Etna, Stromboli and Vesuvius, lie in a straight line.

on the 25th by troop train. We did all the cooking. On the 29th we got there. Then all Hell really began. Inspection every day. Col. Ray was in charge, we went on Bivouac, Rifle Range, hikes, then came the rumor we were to leave soon. So I tried for a furlough. On the 5th of Oct I went to Sacramento. I got a 12 day leave. I saw my wife and son. Gee they were happy. So on the 19th I had Martin Lee Dusa Jr. baptized. So then I had to leave on the 12th. That was the last time I saw Vi and Lee. It was a sad affair. But truly Vi is very good about writing every day.

On the 25 of Sept By troop train we done all the Cooking on the 29th we got there. Then Hell really began Inspection every day Col Roy was In charge, we went on Bivouac Rifle Range Hikes then Come the rommer we were to leave soon, So I tried for a Furlough on the 5th of Oct, I went to Sacremanto I got a 12 day leave I saw my Wife & Son Lee they were Happy so was I on the 19th I had Martin Lee Dusa Jr. Baptized so then I had to leave on the 12th that was the last time I saw Vi + Lee. it was a sad affair But truly Vi is Very good about writing every day.

CAMP BARKELEY NEWS

MRS MARTIN DUSA=

1348 56TH ST SACRAMENTO CALIF=

SWEET WE ARE ON THE MOVE IN A DAY OR TWO DESTINATION UNKNOWN. I WILL WIRE YOU IF POSSIBLE FROM NEW PLACE. ALL IS WELL=

SGT MARTIN DUSA.

CAMPBARKELEY TEX 3   1944-JAN. 3,

Two MRTC Units Reach Full Strength

The 52nd and 56th medical training battalions received their full quota of trainees last week, it was announced by Lt. Col. G. E. Lindow, MRTC executive officer. With the completion of these two battalions the medical training center is now completely organized, he also stated.

Lt. Col. E. J. Browne is commanding the 52nd battalion and Lt. Col. Orlando J. Posey commands the 56th.

this is our's

BATONROUGE LA   1944 JAN 14, PM 3

ALL IS WELL ON TRAIN GOING TO VIRGINIA DONT WORRY WILL WRITE FIRST CHANCE LOVE= SGT MARTIN DUSA

MRTC Mailmen Have Mice, Cookies, Fast Service

By HOMER FERGUSON

Handling the mail service for the whole MRTC every day, without a day off in three months, is no easy job, but that is the work performed by the six men assigned to the medical center's only post office.

These soldiers deliver thousands of letters twice every day to each individual company, send out about 15,000 pieces of mail each day, and give out individually all registered and insured letters. The delivery of mail to each separate company is something unusual for army post offices, for it is usually taken to the battalion or regimental mail orderlies, who distribute it.

Thirty-Six Stops

There are 36 stops on the MRTC mail route and the record time for the truck covering the entire area is only 17 minutes.

In addition to the regular mail, the truck is sent to View three times each week to pick up express packages, in order to save the MRTC boys a trip to town every time these packages are received. An average of about 152 such packages are distributed each week.

Their biggest problem is the forwarding of mail for men who are transferred after their training period is finished. Files are kept for these men and letters are sent to them as long as a month after they have gone.

The post office is not without a pleasant side, and the boys usually manage to get a share of the cookies, cake and candy in the boxes received from home by the trainees.

Doe Gets Mail

The fellows always get a big laugh from the letters with humorous addresses that they receive every day. For instance, a great many letters come addressed to "Pvt. John Doe,——medical training battalion," the dummy address posted in all companies to show the trainees how the folks at home should address their mail. Another letter received was one addressed to a private with the notation, "please hold if AWOL."

The postal soldiers also report they have struck up some interesting correspondence from letters received from girls who feel sorry for the "lonesome" soldiers, and address their letters to "any soldier in Camp Barkeley who wishes to write." The only difficulty, they say, is that these letters always come from girls too far away to call on, however, they afford a nice past-time.

Mice Eat Mail

The boys also have a constant battle with mice, which scurry across the floor, leap in the mail bags, and nibble at letters. Pfc. Leo Allen has become recognized around the office as the official "mouse killer," and whenever one is discovered, it meets a gruesome death under the heel of the "executioner."

One night Sgt. Thomas J. O'Connor, who is in charge of the post office, was working late, and he picked up a mail bag and heard a queer scratching sound in it. Thinking that it was a mouse, and the Sgt. is deadly afraid of the little creatures, he dropped it and left it overnight to let Allen kill the animal.

Allen opened the bag cautiously the next morning and peered in to find that the scratching noise that scared the Sgt. so much was only some cookies which had fallen out of a broken box.

Another time Pfc. Lawrence Cascio was throwing sacks of mail into the truck in preparation for a delivery. He threw one back in and, much to his amazement, it began to move across the floor, leap in the air and perform other such antics heretofore presumed to be beyond the capabilities of a mail bag. He opened the sack with trembling fingers and a little dog stepped coldly out.

Here's Bill Again

A frequent visitor to the post office is Bill, the goat. He has now developed a habit of coming in the back door and going to a wash basin, turning the faucet on with his nose and quenching his thirst.

This practice is all right with Sgt. O'Connor if Bill wouldn't cast such a hungry glance at the letters in the place. The sergeant says that all the letters will have to be put out of sight when he comes in or else Bill will have to find another place to drink.

Soldiers who work in the post office are Corp. William Greider, Pfc. Louis Lombardo, Pfc. Leo Allen, Pfc. Lawrence Cascio, Pvt. Any Lokos and Sgt. Thomas J. O'Connor. Postal officer is Lt. William R. Glasgow.

December 1943

To our Boys in the Service:

In some ways it is hard to realize that another Christmastime will soon be here. For some of you in the service this is the third Christmas that you have been away and for others it is the first.

We have missed all of you more than you will ever know and you can't realize how much we need you now. Needless to say it is our sincere hope that it may not be long before victory will be a reality and that you will again be back with us.

Through the Tiger and individual letters that you have received from the various folks here, you have been kept informed of some of the happenings. Many changes have taken place in the way of merchandise lines and there are many new faces throughout the organization, but underneath it all there is the same old "Gamble Spirit" and the desire to push ahead for new and higher goals. In speaking of the latter just think of the power that will be added when you are all back with us.

This letter will reach many of you in places where you cannot have a Merry Christmas but wherever you are, we want you to know that we are proud of you. While you may be deprived of some of the blessings of the holiday spirit this year, you are sharing in a job which will make possible the enjoyment together in future years the real spirit of Christmas.

It is our pleasure to be able to send you each a little Christmas spending money. We hope you will use it for this purpose and that it may remind you of your many old friends in the organization who send you Heartiest Greetings and Best Wishes for Christmas and the New Year.

Sincerely,

Bert
Phil
GAMBLE STORES

Then things were routine at Camp and I sent home all the clothes I could. So on the 12 of Jan 1944 at 11:30 we were marched to the train. No body knew where; so finally wound up at Camp Patrick Hendy, Va. Gee things were really bad there. British, Italians, Free French and everything a secret, censored mail. Sure a busy place. So on the 15th is when we landed, and on the 21st we boarded the James T. Hill at Hampton Road, Va. There was about 500 of us, things were crowded and cramped. It looked like a slave ship. Eat and sleep and recreation all in the same hole.

Then things were routine at Camp and I sent home all the clothes I could. So on the 12 of Jan 1944 at 1130 we marched to the train no body new where so we finally wound up at Camp Patrick Hendry Va. Gee things were bad there British, Itiations, Free French & everything a secrete censor mail Sure a Busy place. So on the 15 is when we landed, and on the 21st we boarded the James J Hill at Hampton Road Va there was about 500 of us thing were crouded & cramped it looke like a slave ship Eat & sleep & Recreation all in the some hole.

ANOTHER CBI TROOP TRANSPORT · JAMES J. HILL

SAILED JAN. 21, 1944 FROM HAMPTON ROADS PORT, VIRGINIA.

NEWPORT NEWS AND NORFOLK · CITIES ON THIS PORT

APPENDIX "F"

Liberty Type Troopships of Limited Capacity)
(All converted and operated by WSA)

Length, overall ....441' 6"	Gross tons 7,185	Propulsion ....Recip- eng.
Beam .... 56'11"	Speed (knots) 11.5	Passengers....(See below)
Draft .... 27'.7"	Radius (miles) ...17,000	Cargo (cu. ft.) 350,000-390,000

Builders:
  Alabama Drydock & Shipbuilding Co., Mobile, Ala.
  Bethlehem-Fairfield Shipyard, Inc., Baltimore, Md.
  California Shipbuilding Corp., Los Angeles, Calif.
  Delta Shipbuilding Co., Inc., New Orleans, La.
  J. A. Jones Construction Co., Inc., Panama City, Fla.
  J. A. Jones Construction Co., Inc., Brunswick, Ga.
  Kaiser Co., Inc., Vancouver, Wash.
  Marinship Corp. (ex-W. A. Bechtel), Sausalito, Calif.

Except for those few that were fully converted to troopships (see Appendix "D"), the first use of Liberty ships for passengers was following successes in North Africa, when it was decided to bring large numbers of prisoners of war to the United States.

Accordingly, the vessels listed below were nominated for this service. It was planned to carry 308 POW's per vessel—with minor alterations. However, only 113 ships were arranged for 308 capacity by the time it was decided to augment the number to 504.

Of the 113 vessels already converted for 308, fifty-seven remained at that capacity, but fifty-six were altered slightly to enable a load of 504 POW's to be carried. The remaining vessels, which had not yet undergone alteration, went directly into conversion for 504 POW's.

While the Liberty ships so altered were still essentially freighters, it was apparent that (once all prisoners had been transported) a considerable number of U. S. troops could be moved by the large fleet of these vessels. However, somewhat improved conditions were obtained by reducing the berths from "5-high" to "3-high," and making other minor alterations, which reduced the troop-carrying capacity to 350.

The use of ships with this revised capacity had already begun when V-E Day occurred. It was then decided to increase the troop lift of the vessels to 550 each, to assist in the redeployment of troops to the Southwest Pacific. Therefore, alteration work was done on a "no-delay" basis insofar as practicable, 206 of the original list being designated for the increased lift. Work was actually accomplished on but 200, however, inasmuch as six were either lost or did not reach the United States by V-J Day. In the following list, vessels with capacity increased to 550 are unmarked, those not so increased are marked by an asterisk (*) and those lost prior to date of this compilation are marked by a cross (†).

The following Liberty Ships were converted for carrying a limited number of troops:

A. P. HILL
ABRAHAM LINCOLN
ALEXANDER GRAHAM BELL
ALEXANDER LILLINGTON
ALFRED MOORE
AMBROSE E. BURNSIDE
ANDREW FURUSETH
ANDREW HAMILTON
ANDREW MOORE
ARCHBISHOP LAMY
ASA GRAY
BENJAMIN CONTEE*
BENJAMIN HUNTINGTON
BENJAMIN R. MILAM
BERNARD CARTER
BETTY ZANE
BOOKER T. WASHINGTON
BRET HARTE
BUTTON GWINETT
CALEB STRONG
CALVIN COOLIDGE
CHARLES BRANTLEY AYCOCK
CHARLES GOODYEAR
CLARK MILLS*
COLIN P. KELLY JR.*
CONRAD WEISER
CORNELIUS GILLIAM
CORNELIUS HARTNETT
DANIEL H. HILL
DANIEL H. LOWNSDALE
DANIEL HUGER
DAVID G. FARRAGUT
EDWARD BATES*
EDWARD RUTLEDGE†
ELBRIDGE GERRY
ELEAZAR WHEELOCK
ELIHU YALE*
EMMA WILLARD
ESEK HOPKINS
ETHAN ALLEN
EUGENE HALE
EZRA CORNELL
F. MARION CRAWFORD
FELIPE DE NEVE
FELIX GRUNDY
FITZHUGH LEE
FRANCIS AMASA WALKER

FRANCIS L. LEE
FRANCIS MARION
GEORGE B. McCLELLAN
GEORGE BANCROFT
GEORGE DAVIS
GEORGE G. MEADE
GEORGE H. DERN
GEORGE H. THOMAS
GEORGE HANDLEY
GEORGE LEONARD
GEORGE M. BIBB
GEORGE SHIRAS
GEORGE W. CAMPBELL
GEORGE W. McCRARY
GEORGE W. WOODWARD
GIDEON WELLES
GRENVILLE M. DODGE
HANNIS TAYLOR
HAYM SALOMON
HELEN HUNT JACKSON
HENRY BALDWIN
HENRY GROVES CONNOR
HENRY MIDDLETON
HENRY WARD BEECHER
HILARY A. HERBERT
HORACE BINNEY*
HOWARD A. KELLY
IRVIN MACDOWELL
ISAAC COLES*
ISAAC SHARPLESS
JAMES B. RICHARDSON
JAMES BARBOUR
JAMES FORD RHODES
JAMES G. BLAINE
JAMES HOBAN
JAMES IREDELL*
JAMES J. HILL
JAMES JACKSON
JAMES McCOSH*
JAMES MONROE
JAMES MOORE
JAMES RUSSEL LOWELL†
JAMES TURNER
JAMES W. FANNIN
JAMES W. MARSHALL*
JAMES W. NESMITH*
JAMES WHITCOMB RILEY

The sea was rough. I was sick for almost a week, then we saw the Gibraltar and the 12th of Feb we landed in Oran, Africa. We saw many things there that truly brought the war very close. The shot up ships, the docks and buildings. We left by truck to C. P. 2. Area 19. Oh what a place, no lights, no wash water, and tents and C rations. It was cold and dirty there. The boys traded with the Arabs, sold cigs for $3.50 a carton and wine was plentiful and cheap. They got drunk most every night and it would paralyze them. So, I got a pass and went to Oran to see the City. What a place. I was touring the town and at 8 oclock I went to look for the motor pool where the trucks were parked. In my search I got lost so in my search I got in an OFF LIMITS area. The MP's picked me up and took me to the MP station. There I had a Summary Court Martial which cost me a $20. fine and a bust from T4 to a Buck Private. That happened on the 21st of Feb. So on the 27th 2 staff and myself and 2 T 5's went to Florez to some wine as it was Quinlans birthday and we went without a pass. A big PFC MP stopped us before we got in town and asked for our pass.

the sea was rough I was sick for almost a week then we saw the Gibralter and on the 12th of Feb. we landed in Oran Africa we saw many things there that truly brought the war very close the shot up ships the Doks & Buildings we left by truck to C.P. 2. aeria 19. oh wat a place no lights no wash water & tents & C. rations it was cold & dirty there. The Boys traded with the arabs sold cigs for $3.50 a Carton & wine was plentiful & cheap they got drunk most every night. it would peralize them. So I got a pass & went to oran to see the

city what a place I was touring the town and at 8 oclock I went to look for the motor pool where the trucks were parked in my search I got lost so in my search I got in a off Limits aeria the MPs picked me up & took me to the MP Station there I had a Summery cort martial which cost me $20.00 Fine & a Bust from T.4. to a Buck private that hoppend on the 21st of Feb. so on the 27th I Staff & myself & 2 +5 went to Florez to get some wine as it too was a winlens Birthday and we went without a pass and a Big PFC MP stoped before we got in town. and asked for our pass.

Of course we didn't have any so he marched us to the truck and took us about 3 miles to a wire stockade where Italian prisoners guarded us. They too were MP's. Mediterranean Base Section. It was all a big racket, somebody is making a lot of money off the deal as they pick up everybody they can and charge them $25. to a $100. fine. Getting back to the stockade – we spent 4 hours there in the cold so at 11 PM the Company Commander came for our release. He took us to the Camp and called us in the Orderly Room and gave us a lecture on disobeying a direct order. So he asked us if we want a Court Martial or Company punishment. He said you all, as of now, are reduced to the grade of private. But I already was a private so I was afraid he would give me a work out but never said a word to me. So on the 28th (February) we all got ready to leave camp again. We packed up and got on trucks and went to Oran to the docks. We all marched about 2 miles really loaded down and boarded the British ship Landkershire, a troop ship with about 2000 American troops aboard. Then on the 29th

of course we didn't have any so he marched us to a truck and took us about 3 miles to a wire stockade where I station prisoner's Gaurded us they too were the M.B.S. Mediteranian Base Section it was all a Big racket sombody is making a lot of money of the deal as the pull in every-body they can & charge them $25.00 to $150.00 fine getting back to the stockade we spent 4 hours there in the cold, so at 11 P.M. the Company commander come for our release he took us to Camp & called us in the orderly room and gave us a lecture on dis- obeying a derect order. So he asked us if we want a Cort Martial or Company punishment so we all asked for Company punishment, he said you all as of now are reduced to the grade of private But I already was a private, so I was afraid he would give me a work out but never said a word to me, so on the 28th we all got ready to leave comp again we packed up and got on trucks and went to oran to the docks we all marched about we all 2 miles really load ed down and Boarded the British ship Lancashire a troop ship with about 2000 american troops aboard. then on the 29th

LIFE ABOARD the LANCASHIRE   Feb, 28th 1944
                                    March, 7th 1944

Dearest Vi & Lee

Darling How are you and Lee and the Wolfie I am just fine, still aboard the ship. Conditions are not so good, the eats aren't the best and we sleep in Hammocks above our tables we eat on. We wait each day for hours at a time for chow in a line as we have our own pots & pans at each table there are 12 men to a table and we all take turns to go through the Kitchen to get the utinsels filled, which is mostly each day fish and tea. and we get 3 loafs of bread for Breakfast, and four for dinner, and each one thinks he got giped when his share is handed to him. But I don't think it can last much longer, as one of these days we will reach India, we get up at 6 oclock roll up our Hammocks wash and at 7 oclock we eat Breakfast then at 8:30 we have excersizes on A deck. that lastes until 9 oclock. Then at 9 oclock we have Inspection of troop deck E.1. which way up in the front end of the ship. and at 10 oclock we also stand personal Inspection, then at 10:30 we go to a lecture which is held on A deck all about Meleria veneral desiece. then at 11 oclock we get ready for Dinner, at 12 we eat wash our mess kits and go up on Boleck for air and view the sights and at 1:30 we go to another lecture, all about the habits of the natives in India.

then at 2 oclock we are dismissed for the day we wash clothes clean up shower and view the trip write letters, some play cards so shot dice and authers have there mind and thoughts far from where there at, such as mine which are always home with you + Lee. then at 6 oclock we Eat Supper and wash our mess gear. and we have a loud speaker in our hole and they get the news for us from London we all listen to that, of course it too is all put in for the good of the British and Black out orders are put into effect at the same time, no smoking on deck after dark and about 7.30 there is a mad scramble for our Hammocks which are rolled up during the day and piled in a neat pile in the center of our whole. we all manage to get one and put them up. so to releive our feet we take our shoes off and sleep with the rest of our clothes on. as there isent any place to hang them or even lay them down on. But I certianly hope that this living on the water Idea is soon over, it really seems as I Joined the navy instead of the army. But I can manage some how if the rest of the Boys can do it so can I as soon as I reach my destenation I will try and tell you all I can about it. So until then keep your chin up, just as I do mine only living to be with you soon

Yours true Love Martin

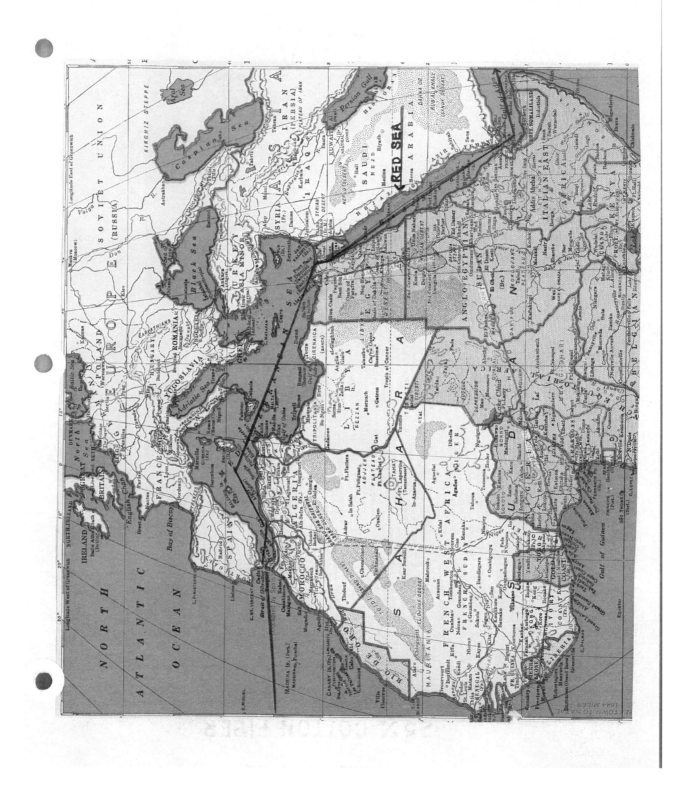

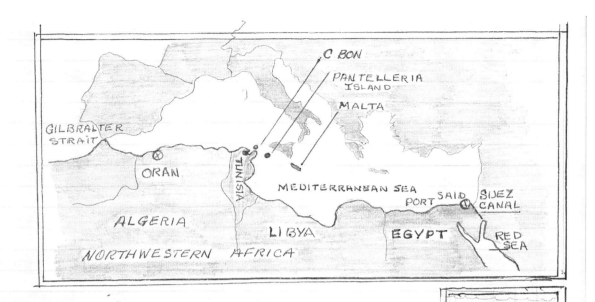

MEDITERRAEAN SEA

SUEZ CANAL

Construction began April 1859. Opened to travel November 1869. Shortened travel distance between England and India by 6,000 miles.

Canal is twice the length of the Panama Canal. It is 103 miles long and has no locks. Travel from Port Said to the Red Sea is 15 hours.

The troop ship Lancanshire anchored over night at Great Bitter Lake. Took on water and food at Port of Suez and anchored again at Port Eden, on the Red Sea.

The Lancanshire departed Oran February 28, 1944 and arrived at Bombay, India on March 20, 1944.

we pulled anchor and started on our journey eastward in the Mediterranean. We had an air raid alarm, no trouble, on the 1st of March. We saw the island of Pantetria, then Cape Bon and then the Isle of Malta, the most bombed spot in the world. The eats are terrible, tea, fish, liver, rice. There are 8 troop ships in our present convoy and in the Atlantic there were 97 ships. On March 6th at 10:15 we got into Port Said. Sure a lot of ships in the bay of the city to the right. We proceeded down the Suez Canal and what a beautiful sight. We anchored in a lake Bitter on the Suez at 6:15. Stayed all night, no black outs, and it looks like a city.

we pulled anchor and started on
our Journey East ward. in
the Mediteranean we had a air Raid
alarm no trouble. on the 1st of march
we saw the Island of pantetria then
cap Bon then the Isle of Malta the
most Bomed spot in the world.
the Eats are terable tea, Fish Liver Rice
there are 8 troop ships in our present
Convoy and in the allantic there were
97 ships on March 6th of 1015 we got
into port Said our sea sure a lot of
ships in Bay the city to our right.
we proceeded down the Suez canal and
what a Beautiful sight we anchored in
a lake Bitter on the Suez at 6:15 PM stayed
all night no Black out it looks like a
City.

MALTA, *MAWL tah,* is a British colony in the Mediterranean Sea about fifty-eight miles south of Sicily. It consists of the island of Malta and four near-by islands.

Malta is the headquarters of the British Mediterranean. During World War II, Malta controlled the vital sea lanes of the Mediterranean Sea. The natural rocks and deep inlets of the island concealed anchorages and submarine bases, and the many underground passages were used as bomb shelters. Malta was heavily bombed throughout the war, but because of the efforts of its gal-

Burton Holmes, Ewing Galloway

The Harbor at Valletta on the Island of Malta is one of the most important in the Mediterranean Sea. During World War II, all Malta was heavily bombed by Axis forces. The port of Valletta was badly damaged, but not destroyed.

Martin Dusa Letter
March 7, 1944

While on board the Lancashire, British Troop ship, somewhere in the Mediterranean

Dearest Vi and Lee,

Darling how are you and Lee and the folks. I am just fine. Still aboard the ship. Conditions are not so good, the eats aren't the best and we sleep in hammocks above our tables we eat on. We wait each day for hours at a time for chow in a line as we have our own pots and pans at each table. There are 12 men to a table and we all take turns to go through the kitchen to get the utensils filled, which is now each day fish and tea. We get 3 loaves of bread for breakfast and four for dinner. Each one thinks he got gypped when his share is handed to him. But I don't think it can last much longer. One of these days we will reach India. We get up at 6 oclock, roll up our hammocks, wash, and at 7 oclock we eat breakfast. Then at 8:30 we have exercises on A deck. That lasts until 9 oclock. Then at 10 oclock we have inspection of troop deck E 1 which is way up in the front end of the ship. At 10 oclock we also stand personal inspection. Then at 10:30 we go to a lecture which is held on A deck. All about malaria, venereal disease. Then at 11 oclock we get ready for dinner. At 12 we eat, wash our mess kits, and go up on B deck for air and view the sights. At 1:30 we go to another lecture – all about the habits of the natives in India.

Then at 2 oclock we are dismissed for the day. We wash clothes, clean up, shower, write letters, and enjoy the views. Some play cards and shoot dice and others have their mind and thoughts from where their at such as mine which are always home with you and Lee. Then at 6 oclock we eat supper, and wash our mess gear. We have a loud speaker in our hole and they get the news for us from London. We all listen to that. Of course, it too is put in for the British. Black out orders are put into effect at the same time, so no smoking on deck after dark. At 7:30 there is a mad scramble for our hammocks which are rolled up during the day and piled up in a neat pile in the center of our hole.

We all manage to get our own and put them up. To relieve our feet we take our shoes off and sleep with the rest of our clothes on. There isn't any place to hang them or even lay them down. But I certainly hope that this living on the water idea is soon over. It really seems like I joined the Navy instead of the Army. But I can manage somehow if the rest of the boys can do it. As soon as I reach my destination I will try to tell you all I can about it. So until then keep your chin up, just as I do mine. Only living to be with you soon.

Your true love, Martin

Today March 7, and 10 AM we started through the Canal and at 1:30 we reached the Port of Suez. We anchored at 2 oclock, took on oil, water and food 2 miles out. The little boats hauled the stuff and 50 air corps men got off and we all sang songs to them. Then the Eqyptians sold gifts from the boats. The MP's wouldn't allow us to buy them. March 8 all set to pull out and at 3:45 we left and entered the Red Sea. 50 men air corp got on and told of their experiences in East Africa. 10 men were with us that their ship was sunk in Nov 12. What an experience they had. 1200 died so they were lucky. March 9 we are in the Red Sea. Not permitted to buy fruit as the natives have a sickness and they don't want the soldiers to get it. It is the plague. It is getting very hot. We are permitted to walk around in our shorts and sleep on the deck. March 13th almost at the end of the Red Sea. At 8:30AM we saw a half sunk ship it truly looked beautiful. We anchored at Port Eden. The city was to the right of us. We stayed all night there too. We took on oil, water, food. On the 14th of March at 5PM we left Port Eden. About 10 troop ships. We all sleep on the floor of the deck. Some stay in the hole and sleep in hammocks strung over our tables, sure hot and stuffy there. Speaking of our 10 ship convoy we had a

today March 7th, at 10 AM we started through the Canal and at 1:30 we reached the port of Suez we anchored at 2 oclock took on oil Water & Food 2 miles out the Little Boats hauled the stuff + 50 air corp men got off. we all sang songs to them, the Egyptians sold gifts from the Boats the MPs wouldn't allow us to buy them, March 8th all set to pull out at 3:45 we left and Entered the Red Sea. 50 new air corp men got on told of their apperance in East africa 10 men were with us that there ship was sunk in Nov 12 what experience they had 1200 died so they were lucky. March 9th we are in the red Sea. not permited to Buy fruit as the natives

have a Sickness and they dont want the soldiers to get it. it is a plage. it is getting very Hot. we are permited to walk around in our shorts and sleep on Deck. March 13th almost at the End of the red Sea at 8:30 A.M. we saw a half sunk ship it truly look Beautiful we anchored at port Eden the city was to right of us we stayed all night there too we took on oil Water Food. on 14th of March, at 5 P.M. we left port Eden about 10 troop ships we all sleep on the floor of the deck some stay in the hole & sleep on Hammocks stung over our tables sure Hot & stuffy there. speaking of our 10 ship convoy we had a

Ex-CBI Roundup
CHINA—BURMA—INDIA
(ISSN 0014-388X)

April, 1989

BOMBAY- WEST COAST ENTRANCE TO INDIA

To the Editor

HOW CROWDED can a street in Bombay be? Pedestrians crowd the shops and the streets.

sub for escort and two destroyers for this damn ship. The water is on half an hour in the morning and some in the evening. On March 15th I pulled guard duty 2 hours on and 4 off, 8 hour shift, still a buck private. Sea of Eden the nights are beautiful, the moon seems close to the water and the stars are so bright. I got acquainted with a nice Indian who is First Cook in the officers mess and lives in Calcutta. He is very good to me, gives me coffee and lunch most always and tells me about India. He says he will come to see me wherever I might be. Today is really eventful day March 17th St. Patricks Day. We all got our stripes back. I got my T4 back.

sub for escort and two Destroyers this dam ship. half an hour in the Eve. on March Duty 2 hrs on & 4 off Buck private. Sea Beautiful the moon the water & the I got acquainted who is first cook and lives in good to me gives me always & tells me he says he will come where ever I might be. really a eventful day St Patricks day we back. I got my

the water is on morning & some in 15, I pulled Gaurd 8 hr shift still a of Eden the nights are seems close to stars. are so Bright with a nice Indian in the officers mess calcutta he is very coffe & Lunch most all about India to see me today is March 17th all got our stripes T 4 Bock

On March 20th 1944 at 5:30PM we docked at Bombay, India. Sure are very busy. Some boys are getting shots, signing payroll, exchanging money for Rupees and mail call. I got 29 letters. Sure a lot of excitement. The Indians are unloading the boat. We didn't get to bed until 11:30. All lights are on. We got up early and dressed into Sun Tans, we all looked sharp. I bought a pair of English jungle pants, shirt, sox for 13 Rupees. Tues March 21st at 7:30 PM we got off the boat and on a train about 100 years old. There were 64 of us in a little old car, one light. Talk about filth and dirt.

on March 20th 1944 at 5:30 PM we Docked at Bombay India. Sure are very Busy some signing pay roll for Ruppees and letters sure a lot of Indians unloading didn't get to bed the lights are on and dressed into look sharp. I Bought Jungle pants shirt tue March 21st got the Boat and on 100 years old there a little old car about filth & dirt. Sure are Boy are getting shots exchanging money mail call I got 29 of excitement the the Boat we until 11:30 cell we got up Early Sun tans we all a pair of English for 13 Ruppees 7:30 PM we got off a train about were 64 of us in one light talk

What is the story of "Rupee Money Belts" that were worn in the CBI?

I had to go to CBI Combat Photographer Garrett Cope of the 10th AF for the answer to this one.

Garrett came up with the above photograph showing two Combat Cameramen wearing the "Rupee Money Belts" that were used in CBI by plane crews and by others.

Silver rupees were sewn into the belts. Also sewn in the belts were a small container of salt and a small container of opium. All those commodities – silver rupees, salt, and opium – were readily accepted by Burmese hill people and Chinese farmers. (Nobody wanted paper money.)

THIRTEEN RUPEES, THE COST OF THE PANTS, SHIRT AND SOX PURCHASED IN BOMBAY
16 ANNAS EQUALS ONE RUPEE
3 RUPEES AND 4 ANNAS EQUALS ONE DOLLAR
10 RUPEES EQUALS THREE DOLLARS & THIRTY CENTS

Troop Train Across India

By James W. Bowman

The 1875th Engineer Aviation Battalion completed the water leg of its deployment to the Far East by debarking at Bombay on Valentine's Day, Feb. 14, 1944. For a week the battalion was quartered at DET CVI Army Air Forces Replacement Center, B.R.D., Worli, and enjoyed the frequent visits to Bombay itself, the "Gateway of India."

On Feb. 20, the unit entrained at Victoria Station, Bombay, for the long trip across country. The following excerpts are from a letter written to my wife at the time, with certain details filled in which had originally been deleted due to censorship:

Boarded a troop train at Bombay and spent the next four days riding across the face of mother India on the Bengal & Nagpur R.R. We were quartered in troop cars with accommodations about as follows: Six men occupied each section; the seats, and the bunks which held them each night were of slatted wood with no cushioning — all you could do was sit and talk, sit and read, or sit and play cards as there was hardly room to get up and walk around, though occasional stops for calisthenics helped keep us limbered up. At one point we stopped along side a village reservoir and half the train stole a swim before we moved on. At every stop we were besieged by all manner of persons — beggars with features and fingers eaten away by leprosy — small dirty children crying, "No, mama, no papa, no brother, no sister" and strangely singing snatches of "Oh Johnny, oh Johnny" — mothers with youngsters on the hip and a basket or jar on the head — all asking for "baksheesh" be it money or scraps of food or cigarette butts. Every stop had a man sharpening knives, bayonets, etc. — his wheel, which was portable, was spun by wrapping a throng around the axle and sawing back and forth on same. The abrasive was supplied by pressing a soft brick against the wheel with one foot. Every station platform was crowded with people waiting tirelessly for some train or other. At one stop we talked through the window with a rather well educated native who I believe was a jeweler, watch repairer or some such — I don't recall just the figures he gave us but for one of his apparent standing his income was still only a fraction of that of a GI. Sometimes a few English kids would show up at the train to try to sell us Indian coins or to beg U.S. coins.

KITCHEN CAR of the troop train was an important part of the train.

The landscape was just a great kaliedoscope of which I recall practically nothing. We did see the ruins of some old forts and temples and I believe saw some Parsee towers of silence as we left Bombay but can't swear to it. Almost a feature of the early morning landscape were the natives squatting about in the fields with their little brass pots performing their daily ablutions.

At the station in Bombay the Red Cross served us tea and cakes and at a night stop somewhere enroute some missionaries did likewise. Otherwise food on the train was mostly canned corn beef, though occasionally they were able to whip up a stew, or oatmeal for breakfast.

The train travelled all night and we were required to sleep under mosquito netting and with head nets as protection against malaria. Every three hours an officer would spray the whole car with an aerosol bomb and wake up everyone to douse themselves with lotion.

WHENEVER the train stopped, there were requests for "baksheesh."

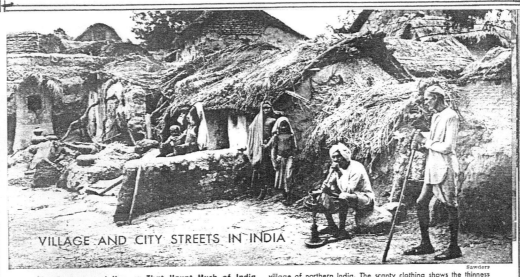

VILLAGE AND CITY STREETS IN INDIA

The Poverty and Hunger That Haunt Much of India are plainly visible in this street of thatched mud huts in a small village of northern India. The scanty clothing shows the thinness of the people, caused by not having enough food to eat.

Between 1800 and 1857 the British East India Company used Indian as well as British troops to wage wars of annexation against Nepal, Burma, Afghanistan, the territory that is now Hyderabad state, and the Sikh state, which included the Punjab and Kashmir. The greed of the Company reduced many of the people of India to poverty and bitterness. The Company was severely criticized in Britain.

Government by Great Britain. After the Rebellion, the people of England felt that abusive rule of India by the East India Company must end. The British Government took over the rule of India in 1858, and power was placed directly in the hands of the British Parliament.

The British Government acquired direct control of all land already governed by the East India Company, plus the territories conquered during the Sepoy Rebellion. All this came to be known as British India.

Consolidation of British Rule. The British Government established its rule over India firmly in the years from 1858 to 1914. Queen Victoria was declared Empress of India at a magnificent ceremony, or durbar, held in Delhi in 1877. The northern boundary of India was established by the Second Afghan War (1878-1881), and in 1885 Burma was annexed to India as a result of the Third Burmese War.

The British installed railroad, telegraph, and telephone systems in India, and rebuilt and enlarged the Indian irrigation system. A system of famine relief was worked out which helped to relieve somewhat the terrible results of India's chronic poverty. The British gained a hold on the affections of many Indian people by their efforts to feed the starving millions during the famine of 1899. But the British Government in India still faced occasional native uprisings and many problems of government and control.

The train stops to feed us as we (don't) have a mess car. There are about 900 of us. At 8:30 that night I though it was a riot. The natives sold knifes and gifts. The next morning, we stopped at Chatigram for breakfast. The Indians all begged for food and boxes meaning give me money or food. March 25, 1944 we had our breakfast at a large junction Nagpur. We are proceeding through jungle, hills and woods. We saw a lot of wild monkeys. Gee the women do all the work and the men lay in the shade, then hustle at night. There was an Indian killed by the train today.

the train stoped we have a are about 900 of us the train stoped a riot the natives the next morning Chatigron for & Indians all bugged meaning give me March 25, 1944 we a large junction proceeding through we saw a lot See the Women do the men lay in fusel at night killed by the train

to feed us as mess car there at 8:30 that night I thought it would sold Knifes & Gifts we stoped at breakfast the kids for food & Boxies money or food" had breakfast at Nagpur. we are Jungle Hills & woods wild Monkeys all the work and the shade there was a Indian today our train

INDIAN WOMEN KEEP BARRACKS (TENTS) CLEAN

Today 8 Engineers got off at a Camp about 3 miles from a village. Well at last the day has come we landed. Today March 25, 1944 we got off the train, got on trucks, and went to Camp about 1 ½ miles away. This city of Krahgpur is a big railroad center. The MP's are pulling town patrol. April 19, things are much the same, we work from 4 AM until 8:15 PM. Very long hours. There are a lot of new soldiers coming in now. Massy, our gas Corporal, got shipped back to the States, he had a bad case of TB. They are putting new straw on our roofs.

8 Engineers got off the train got on to camp about this city of is a Big railroad are pulling down things are much mark from 4 AM Long hours their new soldiers coming our gas corpral got the States he of T.B. they are straw on our

at a camp about 3 miles from a village. Well at last the day has come we landed today March 25, 1944 we got off trucks and went 1½ miles away to Khargpur Center the MPs patrol. april 19, the same we until 8:15 PM very are a lot of new soldiers now Massey shipped back to had a bad case putting new Roofs.

ARRIVAL IN KHARAGPUR, INDIA
MARCH 25, 1944

LEFT — RAILWAY STATION

KHARAGPUR
INDIA

7 FT. 3 INCH COBRA AND
POISONOUS LIZARD
MEN NOT IDENTIFIED

Wing Commander Frank Carey, DFC and two bars to his DFM, a famous Battle of Britain pilot, now in India, shot a leopard while out in a jeep recently. He saw the beast at a distance, stalked it and killed it with his rifle.

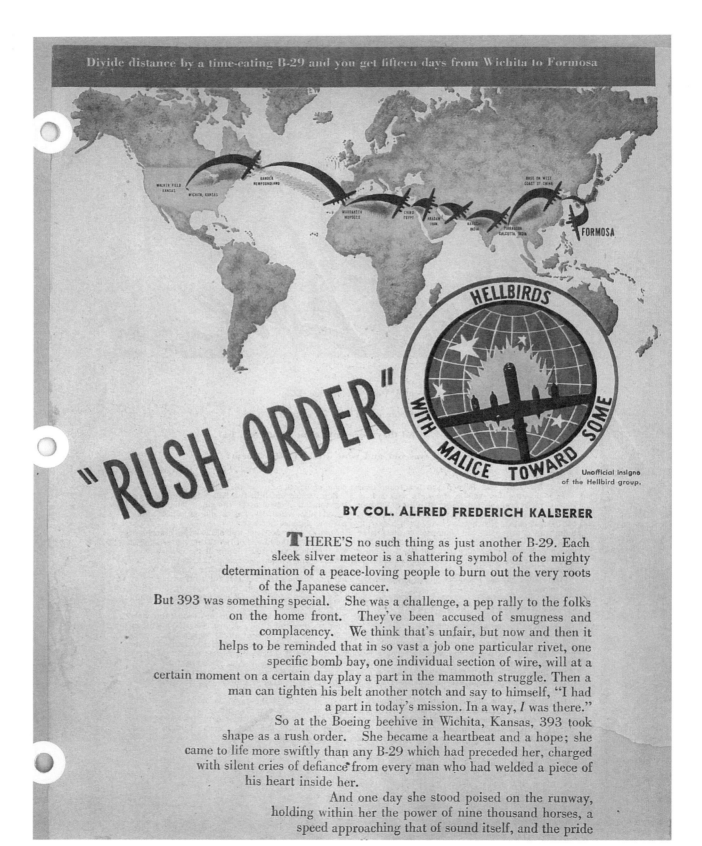

Divide distance by a time-eating B-29 and you get fifteen days from Wichita to Formosa

Unofficial insigne of the Hellbird group.

"RUSH ORDER"

BY COL. ALFRED FREDERICH KALBERER

THERE'S no such thing as just another B-29. Each sleek silver meteor is a shattering symbol of the mighty determination of a peace-loving people to burn out the very roots of the Japanese cancer.

But 393 was something special. She was a challenge, a pep rally to the folks on the home front. They've been accused of smugness and complacency. We think that's unfair, but now and then it helps to be reminded that in so vast a job one particular rivet, one specific bomb bay, one individual section of wire, will at a certain moment on a certain day play a part in the mammoth struggle. Then a man can tighten his belt another notch and say to himself, "I had a part in today's mission. In a way, *I* was there."

So at the Boeing beehive in Wichita, Kansas, 393 took shape as a rush order. She became a heartbeat and a hope; she came to life more swiftly than any B-29 which had preceded her, charged with silent cries of defiance from every man who had welded a piece of his heart inside her.

And one day she stood poised on the runway, holding within her the power of nine thousand horses, a speed approaching that of sound itself, and the pride

Early 58th Wing B-29s
Fought the...

Battle of Kansas

Then on to India and China

By Kenn C. Rust

In preparation for the service advent of the B-29, the 58th Bombardment Operational Training Wing (Heavy) was activated at Smoky Hill, Kansas, on 1 May 1943. In July it was redesignated 58th Bomb Wing (Heavy) and in November 58th Bomb Wing (Very Heavy). By the summer of 1943, the Wing had five groups assigned to it, the 40th, 444th, 462nd, 468th and 472nd (which was subsequently disbanded in April 1944), but it had no B-29s. The first production B-29 was accepted by the USAAF on 21 September 1943, with eleven more being accepted by the end of the month.

On 20 November 1943, a second B-29 wing, the 73rd Bomb Wing (Very Heavy) came into being. The same day, to command the two Wings, XX Bomber Command was activated. Its commander was Brig. Gen. Kenneth B. Wolfe, who had previously commanded the 58th Wing which now came under command of Col. Leonard F. Harman. By 1 March 1944, it had been determined that the 58th Bomb Wing under XX Bomber Command would take its B-29s into action from bases in India and China, and on that day a second bomber command was activated to take the 73rd Bomb Wing into action when bases in the Marianas Islands became available. This was XXI Bomber Command, formed at Smoky Hill, Kansas.

Next, on 4 April 1944, the Twentieth Air Force was activated. It became the first and only Air Force to come into being for the purpose of taking into action a single type of aircraft — a still unproven type at that, the B-29 Superfortress. It was activated at Washington, D.C., and its commander was General of the Army Henry H. Arnold, the commander of USAAF itself.

Meanwhile, the 58th Bomb Wing and its group — all in Kansas with the 40th at Pratt, the 444th at Great Bend, the 462nd at Walker and the 468th at Smoky Hill — were striving to get themselves ready for combat. From August-September 1943, training was constant with an intensive program of classroom instruction, practical maintenance and flying with B-26s and B-17s. Navigators were trained in the medium bombers and bombardiers in the B-17s plus an occasional YB-29. The pilots were experienced officers who underwent additional training in B-26s and then in YB29s and B-29s.

Early in 1944, maintenance groups and ground echelons left their Kansas bases for Ports of Embarkation to begin their trip to India. As they departed, the first of the tactical B-29s began to reach the groups in February. What followed has come to be called the Battle of Kansas, an incredibly difficult struggle to prepare a brand new type of aircraft, still with bugs in it, for combat in a short period of time. It was a struggle made even tougher since the maintenance echelons had departed, leaving only the crews and civilian personnel available to get each plane ready for its flight to war. These men had to effect seven major modifications plus forty to fifty minor ones before a B-29 could be called ready for action. All engines had to be replaced with the "War Engine," and there was an endless fight against time, fatique, confusion and cold weather.

Originally, plans called for 150 B-29s of the 58th Bomb Wing to be ready to start off for India on 10 March 1944. On 9 March, when General Arnold arrived at Salina, Kansas, and asked how many B-29s would leave the next day, he received an all too clear reply. "None." Immediately he issued a string of orders and the Battle of Kansas went into overdrive. All 150 B-29s of the Wing were to be readied and on their way by 15 April. It was impossible, of course, but all restricting red tape was disintegrated and it was done.

In the chill of early morning on 26 March 1944, Col. Leonard Harman climbed aboard his B-29 and led the first flight of B-29s off on their journey to India. They would not be the first of the new bombers to go overseas, however. Early in March, Col. Frank Cook had taken the YB-29 41-36963 to England to give the enemy the impression that the Superfortresses were destined to be employed in the European Theater of Operations.

The first leg of the journey to India took Col. Harman and the other B-29s to Gander Lake, Newfoundland, 2,580 miles. One plane force landed at Presque Isle, Maine. The next leg was to Marrakech, Morocco, 2,700 miles across the Atlantic. It was there the first B-29 was lost. The plane failed to develop enough power on takeoff and crashed off the end of the runway.

From Marrakech, Col. Harman, followed by the others, flew on to Cairo, a distance of 2,350 miles. From there it was 2,400 miles to Karachi and 1,500 miles beyond that to the Calcutta area where the airfields to be used by the 58th's groups were situated. Col. Harman landed at one of these, Chakulia, at noon on 2 April 1944. He was soon followed in by other planes, and by 15 April a total of 32 B-29s had arrived. Some didn't make it. After the Marrakech crash, 42-6350 of the 462nd was lost due to fire on 14 April, and on 21 April, at Karachi, 42-6369 crashed due to fire while 42-6335 cracked up with eight men killed. Both planes were part of the 468th. That made it four planes lost on the journey, and all others enroute were grounded until 29 April while the two Karachi crashes were investigated. Thereafter, the Superforts resumed their flights and by 8 May 130 had arrived at their bases in the Calcutta area.

The fields to which they came were located in flat, hot, bush country and sported concrete runways at least ten inches thick and 7,500 feet long. When the B-29s began arriving, only two fields were operational — Chakulia which was to be the base of the 40th Bomb Group

INDIAN WOMEN carting away dirt and stones during the construction of a 20th AF base in India. Behind them is plane 26229 belonging to the 468th Bomb Group. USAF Photo.

and Kharagpur which was to be the 468th's base. The 462nd's base would be Piardoba and the 444th's base would be Charra. Only, Charra was a mistake, with sloping runways and intense heat. It was nicknamed "Hell's Half Acre" by the Group, and every last man welcomed the day, 1 July 1944, when the 444th moved to Dudhkundi, not far from Kharagpur.

The fields in India were to be the main bases for the B-29s of the 58th Bomb Wing, but their operations against Japan (Operation MATTERHORN) would be flown from forward airfields in China around Chengtu. There were four of these fields, one for each group and each with its own code number. The fields had a single landing strip — 8,500 feet long and 19 inches thick, made of rounded rocks and gravel covered by a native concrete consisting of crushed rock, sand, clay and water — and 52 hardstands. Over 300,000 Chinese worked by hand to build the fields. The 40th Bomb Group would operate from Hsinching, A-1; the 444th from Kwanghan, A-3; the 462nd from Kiunglai, A-5; and the 468th from Pengshan, A-7.

OFFICIAL PAPER OF DOUGLAS COUNTY

4, 1944 — SECTION THREE

Alexandria Man Member of B-29 Bomber Crew in India

Sgt. Martin Dusa Says Super Bombers Worthy of Superman

HEADQUARTERS, 20TH BOMBER COMMAND, AAF, INDIA—One of the most secret of American Air Force bases is the 20th Bomber Command somewhere in India.

Its tales of life there are endless horror, but the immense importance of the work with the B-29 Super Bombers has given the men a sense of really doing a big job.

Dusa

Sgt. Martin Dusa, stationed there in the 86th Service Group of the Ground Forces, has had many flying hours in a B-29 and says they are truly comparable only to Superman.

It takes long hours of ardous work to get the bombers ready for flight, and that unexplainable thrill to see them disappear in the clouds does not go away until every one has returned after a successful mission.

Martin says the most welcome is the cooler weather just arriving there this month, and the disappearance of the malaria mosquito and many other formidable insects. The weather is cool enough for the use of blankets in sleeping.

However, they dare not sleep too soundly or their clothes will be missing in the morning. The Indians steal their trousers to get their watches, pens and wallets, and the boys are not allowed to search them.

Most of the boys hire bearers, native boys, to sweep out their huts and wash some clothing for two ruppees per month. On one trip to Calcutta, Sgt. Dusa paid three ruppees and four annas ($1.08 American money) for two eggs.

S/Sgt. Martin Dusa, who is with the 462nd Bomb Sp. in the 20th Bomber Command, recently has moved to Tinian in the Marianas. June 15 this B-20 group celebrated the anniversary of their first mission over Tokyo. The same day the group received the presidential citation for extraordinary duties performed.

462 ND BOMB. GROUP "HELLBIRD" B-29

On May 1st S/Sgt Laurenthal left our company. He too, had a case of TB. He was our Supply Sgt. Word just came in that we have to move. May 7 we are all packed and boarded a convoy to leave for Peredova about 60 miles away as this is a large B 29 bombing base area. Living in grass huts. The large planes just skim our roof tops on take off. The boys guard bombs and planes and each night they kill a large snake or a tiger. You sure can hear strange noises at night. It sure gets hot here, no breeze at all; 122 degrees yesterday. We have improvised showers we use.

On May 1st S/Sgt Lauenthal left our Co. he too had a case of TB he was our Supply Sgt. and work just came that we have to move May 7th we are all packed and boarded a convoy to leave for Peredova about 60 miles away as this a large 29 Bomming Base aeria living in grass huts the large planes just skim our roof tops on there take off the Boys gaurd Bombs and each night the kill a large snake or a tiger you sure can hear strange noises at night it sure gets hot here no breeze at all 122° yesterday we have improvised showers we use

MAY 7, 1944
B-29 BASE 60 MI.
FROM KHARAGPUR
NO CITY
BASE NAME
PIARDOBA
STATIONED HERE
NINE AND ONE-HALF
MONTHS — UNTIL
FEB. 22, 1945

MY BARRAKS

INDIAN WOMEN AT WORK

Road Work.

There is absolutely no place to go. The nearest town is 137 miles and it is Calcutta so we are stuck in the middle of a swamp. May 15 today I went to sick call. I have been having gas pains. They gave me some pills. It helped some. I also got a letter from Vi. She said on the 26th of April they gave up the house at 1348 58th Street Sacto to leave for Alexandria. Waiting for word to see how they got there. They left 26th of March. Last word I had received today 24th of May is that they were in Fremont, Neb. This has been an exciting day today at 11:30 to the east of us about 12 miles away large clouds of black smoke so the boys went out there and it was one of our B 29's that hit the ground. It had 14,000 gallons of gas and a few practice bombs. So when it hit it tore up the trees and stumps. The pilot got out he tried to rescue some of the men – he drug out 3 and when he went after the fourth the plane exploded. He was burnt so bad he died a few minutes later. 3 gunners burnt to a crisp in a sitting position. All but the tail melted away the aluminum melted there is just absoulutly no place to go the nearest town is about 137 miles and it is Calcutta so we are stuck in a swamp.

May 15. today I went to sick call I been having Gas pains they gave me some pills it helped some. I also got a letter from Vi she says on the 26th of april they gave up the house at 1348-58th St. Sueto to leave for alexandria waiting for word to see how they got there. they left 26th of March. last word I had recieved today 24th of May is they were in Fremont Neb. this has been an exciting day today at 11.30 to the East of us about 12 miles away large clouds of black smoke so the Boys went out there and it was one of our B29 that hit the ground and it had 14,000 gal of gas and a few practise bombs so when it hit it tore up trees & stumps the pilot got out he tryed to rescue some of the men he drug out 3 and when he went after the fourth the plane exploded he was burnt so bad he died a few minutes later 3 gunners burnt to a crisp in a sitting position all but the tail melted away the aluminum melted

The Gurkha Rifleman

By Alan Kyle

The "Military History" magazine in its December 1984 issue contains an article by Byron Farwell titled, "Fierce Johnny Gurk." The following items of particular interest to CBI veterans are extracted from that article.

The Gurkha soldiers from Nepal have served in the British and Indian armies since 1816. These elite infantrymen leave their native land to enlist in military service, and go wherever they are needed throughout the world. Then, when they retire, they return to their native Nepal to enjoy their pensions.

Both the British and the Indian armies still have Gurkha battalions. Those serving the British are now stationed in Hong Kong and in Britain, and the 1st Battalion of 7th Gurkha Rifles fought in the Falklands War in 1982. Prince Charles himself is Colonel-in-Chief of the 2nd Gurkha Rifles.

During World War II, the Japanese overran a British supply dump in Burma, and the Gurkha Guard Detachment there was reported missing. A week later the seven Gurkha riflemen reached British lines, having fought their way through Japanese and thick jungles, carrying the unit's money chest all the way.

A captured member of the 1st Battalion, 7th Gurkha Rifles, escaped from a Japanese POW Camp in Southern Burma, and walked 600 miles in five months to finally reach his lines.

A Bren gunner of the 4th Gurkha Rifles sank with his weapon during a river crossing. Knowing he must never turn lose his weapon, he clung to it until rescuers pried him loose from it and brought him to the surface before he drowned.

Six Gurkhas in Burma in World War II earned the Victoria Cross. One member of the 4th Battalion of the 8th Gurkha Rifles was wounded in a Japanese attack, losing one eye and one hand. He

MEN OF THE 3/10 Gurkha Rifles (23rd Indian Div.) on Scraggy Hill, a point dominating Palel-Tamu road south-east of Imphal. The hill was taken at a cost of 112 Gurkha casualties.

continued to fire his rifle with his left hand for four hours, and later 31 dead Japs were found in front of his position.

The Gurkhas fought against the British in the war with Nepal in 1814, but as mercenaries have remained loyal to the British ever since. They fought bravely and loyally in the Indian Mutiny of 1857, and served in far-flung places in both World Wars I and II, plus many other smaller conflicts.

GUARDS

WATER BUFFLO — A COMMON MAIN DISH IN INDIA

About Mess Halls

● I got a kick out of your Kharagpur mess hall story. That Spam was "something else." Everyone had to eat it, however, but I think many of the mess halls were perhaps better than the one you mentioned.

At the Wellington Barracks mess hall, in new Delhi, the food was usually pretty good. The one at the airport in Agra was better, I think. At least we landed there one time on our way back from Karachi and Bombay, and to our delight they served us fresh milk; all we wanted! Guess they somehow acquired a herd of cattle.

Anyway, what I wanted to say about the Wellington Barracks mess hall was the fact that some of us would take rifles and go out deer hunting a couple times each month. We would bring back six to eight deer, give them to the mess sergeant, then eat good for a month. The deer were quite small, but very tasty.

About the "D" Ration

• Enjoyed the article in the April Roundup about Army food. One ration not mentioned was the "D" ration. It was a bar of semi-sweet chocolate designed to be enough calories for one meal. It was purposely made not sweet so one would not eat it like candy. It was very hard too. I softened mine by leaving it on the hood of the jeep. After a while it became soft enough to eat without breaking my teeth.

The first day we arrived at our India base, Kharagpur, we were introduced to our thatched roof mess hall. Here we had our first encounter with that well traveled item "spam." The mess hall had a blackboard that each day advertised what the entrees inside would be. I remember Chicken Fried Span, Spam A La King, Spam on Toast, and Spam Omelettes. Of course, the eggs in the omelettes were powdered as were the potatoes.

The mess hall was without fresh vegetables, fresh fruit, and of course, no fresh milk. I can't remember what was served for dessert, but do know that we had no ice cream. When ranked with stateside food, this one probably rates a 4.

In April 1945, our crews started the big move from India-China to the Mariana Islands in the Pacific. Our squadron had about 18 planes in flying condition. We had about 23 flight crews. Don't know how it was determined (perhaps by drawing lots), but our crew was selected to travel by troopship to Tinian Island. We boarded the ship in the Calcutta Harbor and spent the next 30 days enroute to the Marianas via Australia. This would be my first experience with Navy chow. Would have to say that it was the best food I would encounter while overseas. There was plenty of fresh meat (of course I mean out of the freezer), fresh vegetables, fruit, good bread and ice cream. Those who appreciated good food thought we had died and gone to heaven.

Food on Tinian reverted to the metal type tray mess hall. Here we were aware of the C-Ration. These rations were housed in fairly large cans. Canned vegetables, fruits, and some meats, etc.

K Rations!

1. It was split into individual meals of breakfast, dinner and supper — thus three packets daily.

2. A five-day drop meant 15 packets and as they were all identical in size and weight — this presented no difficulty when allotting space in one's pack.

3. Every meal varied — and there was sufficient and reasonable choice to satisfy all. It had a high concentrated pork, beef and egg content — usually in the form of a 4 oz. tin per packet — chocolate, sweets, (or candy as the American calls it) — really palatable biscuits, coffee, lemonade, or soup powder and the inevitable chewing gum. Finally, to each packet were four first class American cigarettes (with matches) thus making a ration of 12 cigarettes per day.

4. The calorific value was 4500 daily (or half as much again as we could get from normal scale food, as applied to our own net ration for forward troops).

5. The K ration needed no supplement — it was an ideal answer.

Thus it was. We lived and fought on it for 4½ months — and although latterly one prayed for roast beef and Yorkshire pudding — this "K" ration was deemed a God-sent gift.

ON TROOP SHIPS LEAVING America, across the Atlantic, across Africa, and then on to India. Many of our flights were very long. So, enter the K-Ration! So, what was a K-Ration? Let's see if I remember. There were three varieties. They were marked Breakfast, Dinner, and Supper. They were packaged in a waxy sealed box about the size of a cracker jack box. Maybe 6-7 inches long by 3 inches wide, and perhaps 2 inches deep. Being from the West Coast, I had trouble at first figuring out whether Dinner or Supper was programmed as the last meal of the day. I finally decided that Supper was the one to be eaten at day's end. The K-Ration was designed to be the most food in the smallest package. Therefore, most items inside were condensed or pressed into very hard lumps. Packages contained prune bars, cheeses, crackers, dried fruit, condensed egg bar, etc. One or more of these packages contained a small pack of four cigarettes. Can't remember whether it was Dinner or Supper that contained the cheese, but I always tried to seek that one out.

Food at the various U.S. Air Bases enroute to India was mostly back to the metal tray action and the quality of the food varied from stop to stop.

and made a little river where it ran. No more than 3 foot high of the whole plane was off the ground except the tail. Thousands of rounds of 50 cal ammunition scattered all over the area. One motor here, one over there. It was traveling about 175 miles per hour when it hit. The only one saved was the tail gunner who is in the hospital with a broken shoulder and leg. They say he will live. Gee sure a sad case. Today May 25 some of the boys are going after 35 Gurka guards so probably we won't be here too long at this God forsaken hole. It is an exclusive B29 base. Oh yes, the name of the plane that crashed was "Vivian". June 5, 1944, Here at Priadora there are about 35 B 29's ready to take off on one of the longest bombing missions over Rangoon Thailand and Burma so we are waiting for the results. It has been raining for the past 2 days. At 4:30 this afternoon I went on MP Duty out to the field to keep the runway clear. And we sighted the first Big plane coming in on three motors from Rangoon. It circled the field and a miracle happened. Out of nowhere came a wind storm and dust that you couldn't see your hand ahead of you. I had to lay face down on the runway to keep the wind and dust out of my face and at the same time I was afraid the B29 would crash land. It stormed until 5:30 and it rained. The dust settled and the wind stopped as if a person would shut off a fan.

Gurka gaurds wont be to God forsaken exclusive a yes the name that crashed was (Vivian). at peradova there Ready to tap off Longest Bombing Rangoon & thafand we are waiting it has been raining for the last two days at 4:30 This after noon on MP Duty out to keep the run away clear

so probely me long at this whole it is B29 Base ok of the plane her name June 5, 1944, here are about 35 B29s on one of the missions over Burma to for results raining for the June 5th 1944 noon I went to the field run away clear

am we Sighted plane Comming from Rangoon the field and Happend out of a wing storm you couldn't see ahead of you face down on to keep the wind of my face an time I was B29 would it stormed and it rained the and the wind a person was

the first Big in on 3 motors it Cerculed a merica no where came & dust that your hand I had to lay the runaway wing & dust out at the same afraid the crash land til 5:30 and dust settled stoped as if I shut of a fan

Air Force Sergeant Recalls....

Prison in Rangoon

By William Neugebauer

Ripped open by its own exploding bombs in a bizarre mishap, its tortured engines screaming in metallic agony, the flaming B-29 Superfortress nosed convulsively in a death spin towards the smoky rubble of the Burmese rail center three miles below.

It was early December 1944, and while the guns had fallen silent on the battlefields of Europe, World War II still raged in the far-flung regions of the Pacific, including the China-Burma-India theater.

Former Air Force Sgt. Karnig Thomasian of River Edge, NJ, still recalls the interior "red glow" of the crippled bomber, a garbled crackling over the plane's intercom, his bleeding left hand and bailing out over Japanese-held Rangoon, parachuting mostly headfirst into the hands of enemy soldiers.

B29s in 4th Rangoon Raid

20TH BOMBER COMMAND HEADQUARTERS, INDIA —(P)— A sizable force of B29 Superfortresses smashed at Rangoon today for the fourth time, centering the attack on supply storage dumps on Lake Victoria and the Mingaladon airfield cantonment.

All aircraft returned safely. It was the second blow at the Rangoon area in a week. Resistance was weak.

Rangoon's storage area was bombed with good results.

The B29s were acting in support of British troops which have trapped some 30,000 Nipponese in central Burma. Rangoon was their principal source of supply.

B-29s HIT RANGOON

Marshalling Yards
March 17, 1945

After

MALAGON R.R. YARDS
RANGOON, BURMA

70 planes hit the Malagon R.R. yards. The B-29s were from the 468th BG, 444th BG, 462nd BG, and the 40th BG. All airfields were near the Calcutta area.   EX-CBI ROUNDUP

Before

MALAGON R.R. YARDS
RANGOON, BURMA

"Saigon Sally"?
● Enjoyed your editorial comments on Tokyo Rose last issue but up in Assam the gal we listened to we called Saigon Sally. She kept us posted on that big flight of Curtiss Commandos from the time they left the States until they arrived in India and was always telling us about the infiltrators they were dropping in to our area. Was it Rose or Sally?

The Jinx story was wonderful. I came in at the end sentence at Calcutta when Pat O'Brien had me take the girls in town to buy shoes at Batas. I took Pat to a busy burning ghat on the Hooghly and he almost got sick. I took Jinx's picture here for the paper a few years back when she was doing promotion for the gas industry and she remembered every detail of our going through the hospitals in Calcutta. Quite a gal.

How's Your CBI IQ?

Questions This Time Instead of Answers!

Who was "G.I. Jill?"
Bill McClenachan, Tenth AF AACS, remembers listening to "GI Jill" on Armed Forces Radio. Bill is now at 87 Sunset Dr., New Hope, PA 18938.

"She was a welcome relief from Tokyo Rose," Bill says. He recalls her airwaves signature as approximately the following:

"Good Morning to some of you. Good Afternoon to some of you. And to the rest of you, Good Night."

Bill would like to know "G.I. Jill's" real name and where she is now.

Can any of our readers provide an answer?

+ + +

TOKYO ROSE was actually a UCLA graduate who performed propaganda work to a factory assembly line.

Tokyo Rose a Help?
● Read the article in your December issue concerning Tokyo Rose. I didn't think it was very nice. I know she did propaganda during the war, but some of us enjoyed hearing her broadcast while we were in India and Burma. We learned more about what was going on from her than we did from our own armed services radio. Like the time we were bombing Okinawa. She told us about that five days before the Americans even admitted it. She also told us about the surrender of Japan before American radio. Also, we liked to listen to the American records she played. And, she wasn't as nasty as Axis Sally and Lord Haw Haw who broadcast from Germany. I felt that I just had to get this off my chest.

Editor's Note:

Joe, I certainly was not as entralled with Rose as you were! She tried very hard to destroy the American soldiers' morale. She told of the uselessness of continued fighting on their part. She also told of non-support on the home front, and intimated that wives and girlfriends in the US were not exactly waiting for us to come home. No Joe, records or not, I was not thrilled with her.

How Did Tokyo Rose Know?
● Read with interest the letter by Homer Whitmore in the Roundup as to how Tokyo Rose knew about plans to move the Chinese Army. While stationed in Kweilin, I found this out. We had heard in town one night that our full group of B-24s would be stopping for us to gas them up for a raid on Formosa. Our base CO didn't get notification 'til the next day when they were about 20-30 minutes out. So, questions were asked and apparently one of the Eurasian girls in town knew about it. These girls spoke about 4-5 languages and did a lot of listening. As a result, 13 very beautiful Eruasian-Jap girls were arrested by the Chinese and traitor signs were hung around their necks. They were then taken out behind a hill on the edge of town and shot. A couple of the girls had radio transmitters on their person. They sent messages to Japan two or three times per day. The Japs knew most of our outfits name, etc. Also house boys had been picking up letters from home written by parents, wives, and girlfriends. These contained information that could be passed on to Rose about certain guys' families. I would like to know how many times she scooped our armed forces.

As soon as it cleared the planes started coming in. One landed every six minutes. But our three motor job had to land at Visazepur on a fighter strip and it isn't long enough to take off on so they had to take the whole plane apart and haul it here piece by piece. June 6, 1944 Just heard that the second front started in La Harve, France. 11,000 planes, 4000 ships and some 2000 smaller ones. And 5000 troops took part. Everyone here just went wild with joy.

> as soon as it planes started landed every But our 3 photo land a Visa fighter strip long enough to they must plane apart here by P.M. 1944 Just heard second front La Harve France 4000 ships + smaller ones took part we just went joy.
>
> cleared the coming in one six Minutes Job had to repair on and it isent to take off on must take the and haul it ces. June 6th started in once 11000 planes some 2000 and 5000 troops one here will with

Planning for the big invasion was begun in 1943 under direction of General Dwight D. Eisenhower. More than two million American and British troops were massed in the British Isles for the great attack. Sixteen million tons of arms, munitions, and equipment were stored up, ready and waiting. Four thousand ships and landing craft, including sixty types built especially for the invasion, were on hand. And eleven thousand planes were ready to give protection overhead.

Large-scale bombing of the French coast began three months before the invasion. Bombs were dropped not only at the intended landing places, but at other possible points of attack, so that the Germans could not guess where the invasion would take place.

D-Day. Twenty hours before the invasion began on "D-Day," hundreds of Allied bombers attacked the batteries, command posts, and control stations in the proposed landing area. Parachute troops went ahead of the invasion forces to cut railroad lines, blow up bridges, and seize landing fields. Gliders followed the paratroopers, bringing in men, jeeps, light artillery, and small tanks. By this time the great invasion fleet was on its way from Great Britain to the coast of Normandy, in northern France. Allied battleships fired two hundred tons of shells a minute toward the Nazi coast batteries. A half hour before the first landing on June 6, 1944, two thousand tons of bombs were dropped on the Normandy beaches.

Then the Allied troops waded ashore. British and Canadian forces landed near Caen, and pushed inland to capture Bayeux. United States troops landed on both sides of the Vire River.

Within five days the Allies had landed sixteen divisions and seized eighty miles of the coast of Normandy. They went on to take a large part of Normandy, and then began to pile up supplies for a great offensive on French soil. The Allies in France used man-made harbors until the port of Cherbourg was captured.

The "Break-through." The capture of St. Lô on July 18 opened the way for the Allies to break out of Normandy and push on across France. On July 25, three thousand bombers and a vast number of heavy guns began bombarding a section of the German line west of St. Lô. On that day and the next day, infantry and tanks followed up this preliminary attack, and succeeded in cutting through the German lines. Tanks raced south into Brittany and down to the Loire River. Another column of Allied troops headed east, directly toward Paris.

The Germans tried to counterattack. But British and Canadian troops broke through at Falaise to meet the United States forces and close a trap around the German Seventh Army. That army was destroyed in four

NORMANDY INVASION — D-DAY

Hitting the Beach. United States infantrymen storm the Normandy beachhead after dropping from the bows of an invasion barge. They crouch under the weight of full packs and rifles as they wade waist deep in the rough waters of the English Channel toward enemy positions on the shore. The invasion of Normandy by the Allies began June 6, 1944.

Coast Guard, U. S. Navy

Anxious Eyes. On the bridge of the U.S.S. Augusta, part of the Allied invasion fleet, United States Navy and Army officers watch the progress of the invasion forces on the shore.

Objective Won. Admiral Harold R. Stark leaves a Nazi gun emplacement which was knocked out by naval shellfire on the shore of France during the opening stages of the invasion.

Supplies for the Battle of France. After the fighting had moved inland, the Normandy coast was still a busy place as thousands of ships scuttled back and forth from England, supplying the Allied fighting forces with food, ammunition, and fuel for the armored divisions. This task was to last from invasion to final victory.

They are all singing "I'll be home for Christmas". Oh yes, from our Rangoon and Thailand raid we didn't lose a plane and no opposition was encountered. Well, Well. June 15, 1944 At 10:30 PM the B 29's bombed Japan on the morning of the 13th. I was on guard duty at the end of the runway to see the planes take off. It was a sight to see those Big Babys take off all loaded down for Japan. Four planes took off. The fifth was about half way down the runway coming at about 185 miles per hour and a door flew open. The speed tore it off and a rubber life raft came sailing out and most of its contents came rolling up to me. But the raft itself got stuck in the rods on the tail of the ship. But he couldn't stop as he had to get into the air. He was near the end of the runway so he circled the field and I thought that he would blow up as he was loaded. But the pilot and co-pilot had a hard time to bring the nose down.

they are all
home for Xmas
from our
raid we
a plane &
encountered.
June 15, 1944 at
B29's Bomed
morning of the
Toura at the
away to see
tape off it
to see those
of all loaded
Japan four pla
the 5th ones
half way down

singing I'll Be
). A yes for our
Rangoon to Hanjok
Didn't look
no opposition
Well well.
10:30 PM the
Japan on the
B. I was on
end of the run
the plane
was a sight
Big Babys tape
down for
nes took off
was about
on the runaway

coming at about
hi send a d
and the speed
and a rubber
sailing out
Contents come
me. But the
got stuck in
the tail of the
he couldent
get into the door
the End of the
so he circuled
I thought that
up as he was
pilot & co pilot
to Bring the

at 185 miles per
oar flew open
tore it off
life raft come
and most of its
rolling up to
raft it self
the rods on
he ship. But
p cy he had to
he was near
runaway
the field and
he would blow
loaded But he
had a hard time
nose down.

We stood there afraid with our mouths open. But thank God he made it. Last week one burned up when they were refueling with gas. It is a million dollars when one of these melt and I mean melt. No one was hurt. Col Carmichael led the formation from here. He is our Post Commander. And General Wolf is our Commander of the 20th Bomber Command. We are in the 462 Bombing Group which bombed Japan. There were some with bullet holes but it sure was good to see them come back.

we stood there
our mouth
God he made
one Burned up
refulling with
little over. a
when one of
many melt.
hurt. Col.
our formation
no our port
and Gen Wolf
of the 20th Bom
we are in the
which Bomed
some came back
holes in But it
to see them
afraid with
open. But thay
it last week
when the were
gas. it is a
million dollars
those melt I
no one was
Carmichel be
from here he
Commander
is our Commander
our Comand
462 Boming Grop
Japan. there were
with Bullet
sure was good
Come back

PILOTS AND GROUND CREWS here are shown "sweating out" the return of a flight of their PLANES from a mission. One of the aircraft, which has been successfully "sweat," taxis to a dispersal area. EX-CBI ROUNDUP

There are rumors here that all of us fellows that are in the XX (Twentieth) Bomber Command will issue us the Soldiers Medal of Honor so we are waiting to see. The weather has been hot. It was 118 degrees in the shade. One boy died of heat stroke this morning. Sunday June 18. We all have the heat rash really bad. June 23. We have just had our first real air raid, some AA fire and all. But where we were in the foxholes we couldn't see anything. It lasted over an hour. Today we also got our APO No. changed to 220. First our order was 0995G and then APO 9468 then when we got to Bombay it was changed to 493 then to 220 which means another move soon. Yes, today June 25, 1944 the 1280 M. P. Co. has ceased to exist. We are still all together. 71 men and Lt. Voss and Lt. Gervin are to stay here at Priadora and join up with the 25th Repair Sqd as guards and the cook. 29 of us are going some place; destination or organization still unknown. We are all transferred in grade. First Sgt Sanderson, Sgt Zeltzer, Cpl Young, Cpl Brown and a few others.

there are roomers here that all of us fellows that are in XX Bomer comand will Issue us the soldiers Medal of Honer so we are waiting to see today the weather has been 204 it was 118° in the shade one Boy died of heat stroke this Morning Sunday June 18th we all have the heat rash. reall bad. June 23. we have just had our first real air Raid some AA Fire an & cell. but where we were in foxholes we couldent see any thing it lasted over a hour. today we also got our AP. #no

changed to 220 first our order was 0995 J. then APO 9468 Then when we got to Bombay it was changed to 493. Then to 220: which means another move soon. yes today June 25, 1944. the 1280 M.P. Co. Hay Arone to Egypt. we are still all together 71 men & Jt Voss & Jt Gervin are to stay here at peradova and join up with 25th Repair Sq. as Gaurds. and the Coop 29 of us are all going some place Des tenahon or Erginogle still unknown we are all transfered in grade 1 Sgt Sanders Sgt Zeltzer Cpl Young Cpl Brown. + a few outhers.

The Battle With Annie

seriously. A member of the 835th Signal Service Battalion at Bangalore thought they never had it so good despite the general fruitfulness of this frightful insect.

"The mosquitoes are big enough to stand flat-footed and kiss a turkey," one 835th GI wrote home, "but they aren't Annies and don't give us much trouble. We're on per diem, and mess at the West End Hotel is good."

The Japs apparently didn't take them seriously enough, either. They lost the battle of Pingka in China to the malaria-bearing mosquito and typhus-bearing chigger. Annie and her allied mites won where the Chinese failed to dislodge the Nips' first-rate fighting team. When the Japs tried to invade India at Imphal, they lost 44 out of every 100 men they had. Around 65,000 Japs and their 17,000 horses perished, more from disease than from battle, and malaria was one of the leading killers.

The first organized malaria control and survey units arrived in CBI in early 1943 to beef up the war against the mosquito. They faced forces more numerous and formidable than those of the Japs. Medics in India and Burma knew, if Americans didn't, that malaria, outside of nutritional intestinal plagues, was the chief menace. These first units didn't achieve spectacular results because mosquitoes and their breeding sites were much too numerous. Also, these first units lacked two formidable weapons, atabrine and DDT. Two malarial control detachments went with Allied troops when they reentered north Burma in the fall of 1943, but they soon found there was a great degree of impracticality to malaria control for troops on the move. As time went on, the control surveying and eradication increased, four malaria control detachments beginning CBI work in the fall of 1944.

To begin the job of controlling malaria in an area, a survey unit laid the groundwork for a control unit. The survey unit, consisting of two officers, an entomologist and a parasitologist, plus 11 men, evacuated areas and examined the blood and spleens of local children to determine incidence. The control units had one officer and 11 enlisted men. They drained areas, sprayed, and mosquito-proofed quarters.

Colonel Haas, the mosquito troops' leader, in attacking the highest malaria rate on earth, secured millions of yards of hessian cloth. This cloth, made from jute by India's textile mills, was used in bamboo bashas, tents, bombed buildings, or anything else the Army used as a billet. Haas furnished along with his mosquito netting his customary advice about wearing complete uniforms at night and using insect repellent and aerosol bombs when available.

Prickly Heat Enjoying Vogue In CBI-Land

By S/SGT. KARL PETERSON

Enjoying quite a vogue with American service personnel in India this season is that dear old friend prickly heat, heat rash, Asiatic crud, or "that (censored) (censored) (censored)." Terminology varies with the severity of each individual's case. Found especially in large urban areas, this modern people's plague democratically strikes high and low, mighty and minion.

Crusading as ever for the welfare of all CBI dog tag wearers, therefore, the rampant *Roundup* this week sent its learned medical editor to the local station hospital for some pukka gen on causes, effects and cures (if any.)

The disease, it seems, has almost 100 per cent incidence in severe areas, but mortality is negligible, if not nil, so it ranks as a pest rather than a killer. This excludes cases of guys being run down by lorries while engrossed in scratching, or asphyxiated by choking clouds of heat rash powder.

Prickly heat, technically, is a skin irritation. What causes it, Mr. Bones? Well, technically, we sure as hell don't know. There are theories—and theories. One is that the old hide is rankled by the dried salt of previous perspiration ... logical enough.

Effects, on the other hand, are definite, violent, and strictly to type. An attractive red blotchy rash, like strawberry hives, covers your carcass, from toenails to hairline, centering on the inside of the arm joints, armpits and—er, other friction areas. The victim then starts itching, bitching and twitching, develops a temper like a well-teased Bengal tiger and bags under the eyes from nights of whirling, dervish fashion, on a figurative bed of nails.

For surcease of these afflictions, there are literally hundreds of cures, all worthless. G.I. dispensaries offer calomine lotion and prickly heat powder, the latter containing zinc oxide, starch, boric acid and camphor. Calomine, liberally slapped on the torso, dries quickly to a coating of zinc oxide also, leaving you all powdery white like a bagman in a flour factory. These are mere palliatives, however, skin-driers, and the lad who returns to his sweaty toils after treatment is soon prickly again.

Anything which stops perspiration is to the good, lying quietly and nakedly on one's bunk taking it easy brings relief, usually, but some say there are already too many India-based troops so engaged, and there is a war on, y'know.

Medical authority has two more ideas. Don't use soap in showering more than once daily, it exaggerates skin irritation; and get a little sun tan to toughen the skin. For go'sakes, however, cry the docs, don't go all out in one day on this sun business; leisurely one-hour snoozes beneath the scorching Indian sun will turn out a line of burn cases that will make heat rash a pleasure to recall.

The medics, therefore, say only cool weather can cure; others are not so modest. Pukka panaceas, mixtures of rice pannee, betel nut and G.I. coffee are whispered about as sure-cures. One Filipino-American friend of ours named Llewellyn swears by *Skat*, the popular mosquito repellent.

CBI-men at large, however, await a modern Pasteur who will unearth a swift and certain cure for the malady. To his fame will be erected, by the grateful masses, a second Taj Mahal, the size of The Pentagon.

Friday July 7, Well Well the boys took off yesterday and today we got reports that the second bombing of Japan by our supers. Case Ace, King Size, Old Bitch, Uarsy Best, Star Duster, Big Chief and a few others. The raid was successful. No loss to our planes. We are sure doing a big job. Well a long time has past and many things di happen on the 25th of July. We broke up. I was transferred to the 86th Service Group and then put on the D. S. to the officers mess in charge of 16 cooks and KP. We feed 85 officers.

Friday July 7th Hallowell the Boys took off yesterday & today we got reports that the Second Bombing of Japan By our Supper fortress was a King Size old Bitch u any Bess, Star Duster, Big Chief, and a few others, the raid was successful. no lost to our planes we sure are doing a big Job. Well a long time has past and many things did Happen on the 25 of July we broke up at M.P. I was transferred to 86th Service Sq. then put on D.S. to the officers Mess in charge of 16 Cooks & KP. we feed 85 officers

CREWMAN LEANS OUT OF EXTENDED B-29 NOSE, DISTINGUISHED FEATURE OF THE NEW PLANE

MEN TURN PROPELLERS BEFORE B-29'S MOTORS ARE STARTED. HOFFMAN FLEW IN THIS PLANE

PLANES ARE BOMBED UP BEFORE RAID. ALL OF THEM GOT BACK WITH SPARE GAS

B-29 SUPERFORTS BOMB JAPANESE MAINLAND
NEW U. S. WARPLANES FLY FROM CHINESE BASES TO HIT YAWATA, THE PRIME JAPANESE STEEL CENTER

On June 16 (Tokyo time) the U. S. Army Air Forces began to use a weapon with which it had long threatened Japan. Employing the most powerful bomber in the world, the Boeing B-29, it started the strategic bombing of the Japanese homeland. Unveiling its long-secret giant of the skies, in the works since 1936, the Army revealed that this Superfortress can fly faster and higher than the famous Flying Fortress (B-17) with a much heavier bomb load, shoot at attacking planes from remotely controlled turrets. On its first mission its performance was highly satisfactory. Hampered by the necessity of flying all bombs and fuel over the "Hump" from India to China, the first raid was but a token of what will surely come. For with the lessons learned in Europe, where strategic bombing has had to relinquish its priority to tactical bombing since the invasion, U. S. fliers are eager to prove with their new weapon that an enemy country can be crippled and killed by attacks from the air.

The first blow hit the Japanese where it hurt most. As these pictures by LIFE Photographer Bernard Hoffman show, the behemoths took off from bases in China which had been hand-built by 360,000 coolies in a few months. They flew to the southernmost island of Japan, Kyushu. There they cascaded high explosives on Yawata, the Far East's Pittsburgh, which produces a fifth of all Japan's steel. One plane was lost in the intense anti-aircraft fire over the target and three others failed to return from the raid. As they headed back toward China, crews could see fires rising into the night sky, visible for more than 60 miles.

Japanese spokesmen belittled the damage done but an extraordinary session of the war cabinet obviously considered the attack with more gravity. Now all Japan, in whose small land area industry is crowded together, lies open to aerial attack. Her coastal fleet, released to haul booty from conquered lands, will probably have to be recalled to help the over-burdened railway system which can be smashed at key points.

Two Local Men Radar Operators in Bombardment Wing

58TH BOMBARDMENT WING, TINIAN—With the end of the war against Japan and the removal by the War Department of the veil of secrecy which shrouded the use of radar equipment, announcement has been made by the 58th Bombardment Wing of the combat crewmen who served as radar operators in the Superfortress onslaught against Japan.

Among these "unsung heroes" of the 58th Wing who played such an important but little-heard-of role in the Superfortress blitz on Japan were Second Lieutenant Robert E. Nelson, Route 5, Alexandria, and Staff Sergeant Edward L. Swart, Route 1, Osakis.

The B-29 was the first plane to carry a radar operator as a regular member of every crew and, although these men received little recognition during the war because of the "security blackout" on their activities, they largely contributed to the outstanding record of bombing accuracy established by Brigadier General Roger M. Ramey's pioneer Superfortress unit.

Figures released for the first time by Captain Henry Young of Frankfort, Ky., radar operations officer, show that bombing was performed by radar on 51 per cent of the missions conducted by the 58th Wing from Tinian. An outstanding example of the effectiveness of this type of bombing is indicated by the results of an attack on Numazu on July 17, when 112 out of 119 bomb releases were made by radar and caused destruction of 89.5 per cent of the target area.

On daylight missions, when the target was obscured because of weather conditions, it was the radar operation who determined when to drop the bombs, and during the devastating night incendiary attacks, radar men in "pathfinder planes" made the first bomb releases and started fires which served as a guide to the following Superforts.

These men also played an important part in navigation of the big bombers on the long flights to every part of the Jap empire, locating island check points, obtaining wind and grounds speeds, spotting flak areas and checking on weather fronts for thunderstorm activity. Equipment used by these men made possible the many outstanding feats of bombing and navigation but it was the skill of the operators which determined the effectiveness of the equipment.

B29s Score Well in Raid on Singapore

WASHINGTON—(LP)—A medium force of India-based B29 Superfortresses achieved "good results" in a daylight raid on enemy shipping installations at Singapore, the war department announced.

Tokyo radio already had reported damage to military installations at Singapore, as well as destruction of 20 or more civilian dwellings and "scores" of casualties.

Gen. Henry H. Arnold, commander of the army air forces, announced in a Twentieth air force communique that none of the giant bombers was lost to enemy action in the Singapore raid. The American airmen, he said, shot down four enemy aircraft, probably destroyed another and damaged 12.

Arnold also announced further checks revealed two B29s are missing and believed lost as a result of enemy action during the Tuesday night raid on Tokyo by Saipan-based Superfortresses.

He said the raiders on this occasion destroyed 14 Japanese fighters, probably destroyed three others and damaged nine.

The Singapore raiders were from Maj. Gen. Curtis E. Lamay's 20th bomber command.

Another Japanese broadcast said lone Superfortresses from the Marianas made three nuisance raids on Tokyo itself between 9 o'clock Wednesday night and 2:40 a.m. today, dropping fire bombs but causing no damage.

The raid on Singapore was the second by the 20th bomber command. Last Nov. 5, another force of the huge four-engined raiders scored hits on a drydock and wrecked other installations in the strongest naval base in southeast Asia.

The Tokyo radio claimed two B29s were shot down and 14 others damaged, two of them also probably destroyed today.

B29s HIT SINGAPORE
Jap base bombed in daylight

THEY DIRECTED THE BOMBING OF JAPAN—These officers of the AAF carried out the attack on Japanese industrial targets when the new B-29 super-bombers made the memorable raid and received their baptism of fire. Left to right, Brigadier General Kenneth B. Wolfe, commanding general, 20th Bomber Command; Brigadier General John E. Upston, assistant chief of staff; Brigadier General Laverne G. Saunders, wing commander.

my friends

NEW B-29 SUPER-FORTRESS IN FLIGHT—The entire globe is the battle area of the long-range bomber of the U. S. Air Force which received it baptism of fire in the memorable attack on an industrial center of Japan. Capable of carrying a heavy load of bombs over a long distance, the great ship can do well over 300 miles an hour and has a ceiling of more than 300,00 feet. It is powered by four 18-cylinder radial air-colled engines of 2,200 horsepower each. Inset, badge of the 20th Air Force, the newly created global command.

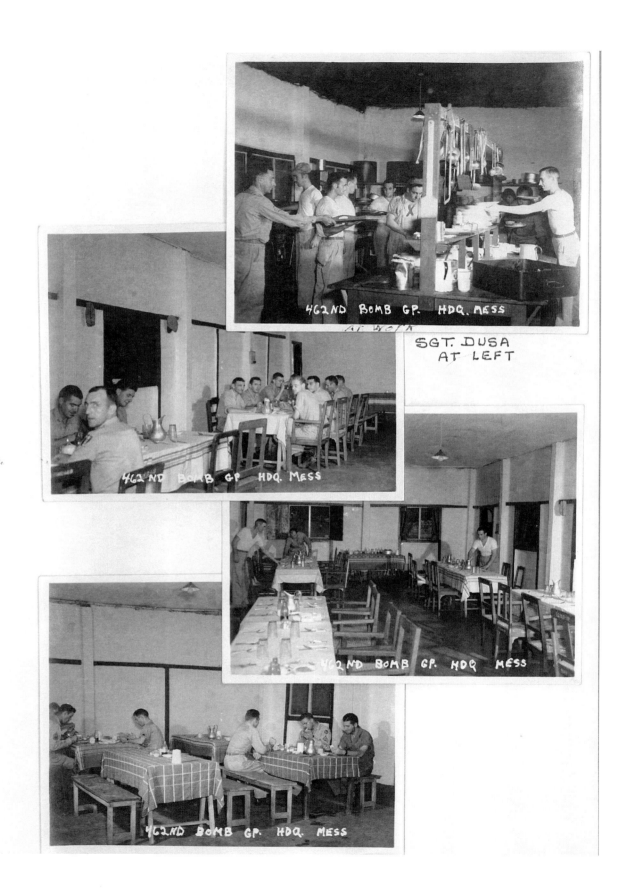

MAJ. RASSON
COL. LOWBERG
MAJ. FAUSETT
COL. STORRY
COL. HOISINGTON
COL. ROUSH
PVT. McCAFFERY, TOM
     LOWELL, MASS.
SGT. DUSA, MESS SGT.

VIC
OWENS
WILSON
FOLEY
HAHN, JOHN
DUSA
MONSOON

TOP- OFFICER'S MESS

CENTER
MESS CREW
SGT. DUSA IN CHARGE

LEFT- NATIVE BOYS
      K-P DUTIES

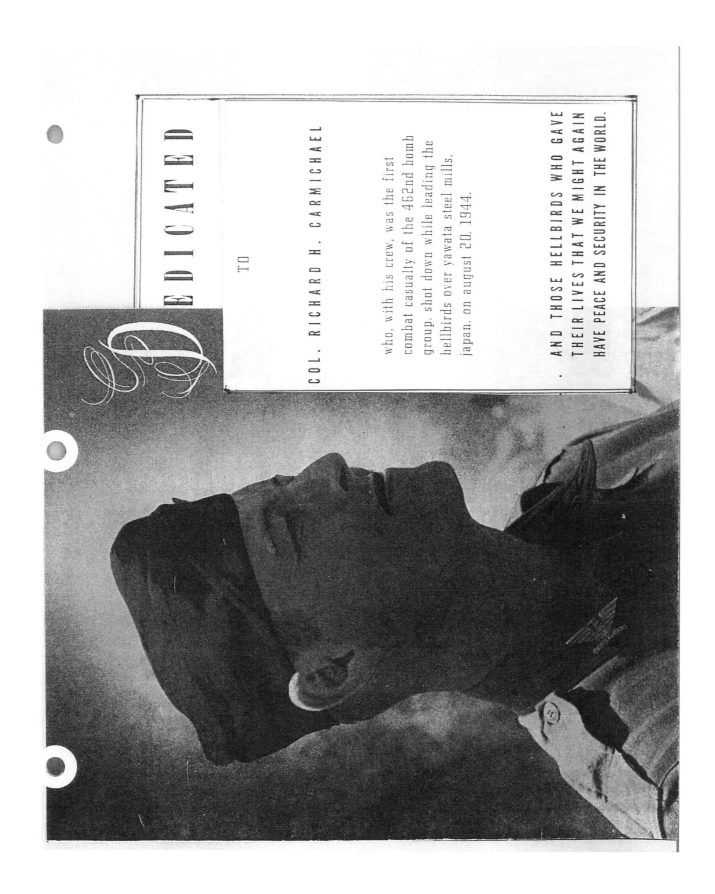

DEDICATED

TO

COL. RICHARD H. CARMICHAEL

who, with his crew, was the first combat casualty of the 462nd bomb group, shot down while leading the hellbirds over yawata steel mills, japan, on august 20, 1944.

AND THOSE HELLBIRDS WHO GAVE THEIR LIVES THAT WE MIGHT AGAIN HAVE PEACE AND SECURITY IN THE WORLD.

We opened it on August 12th. On the 20th of August many of our officers including Col. Carmichael was lost over the target on the 22nd. A B29 cracked up just ¼ mile short of the runway, killed two and wrecked the plane. I am still a Buck Sgt waiting to make Staff. Well here it is the 27th of Sept. On the 14th of Sept me and Ralph Ravelli went by truck in the back end we rode for 12 hours; then we reached Calcutta where we went on business. I got some stuff for the officers mess and the NCO Club and Ralph got stuff for the Club.

we opened it the 20th of Aug officers Including he was lost on the 22nd just 1/4 mile short killed two plane. I am sgt. waiting Well here it is 14th of Sept I by truck in rode for 12 hrs Calcutta where buisness I got officers mess and and Ralph got august 13th on many of our Col Carmical over the target a B29 cracked up & run away & wreaked the still a Buck to make stuff 27th Sept on the & Ralph Rovelli went the back End we then we reached we went on some stuff for the N.C.O. Club stuff for the club

CALCUTTA STREET SCENES -
'SACRED COWS'

BAREFOOT SHOPPERS

CALCUTTA:

METROPOLIS OF MISERY

FORMER BRITISH OFFICERS (still excluding Indians from their clubs) insist Calcutta is the most beautiful city in the world. To the masses of natives who live, and die, on its streets, it is a different thing. No one knows how many are the homeless and miserable, but estimates run from 400,000 to a million—a great sea of beggars and cripples, of the hungry and dying. Among them are the tragic uprooted victims of the war which divided India and Pakistan. Baked by the same tropical sun and soaked by the same monsoon rains, these Moslems and Hindus are the debris of bitter religious difference. Their anguish is exploited by Soviet agents and local demagogues, but it is none the less real in this crowded city, the world's greatest metropolis of misery.

This fortunate beggar owns a hollowed gourd for the food he scavenges, and a battered umbrella. All else is lost: his family, his home, his youth and his hope. His face looks forward and sees only the past.

TAJ MAHAL IN AGRA, INDIA

BUILT IN 1635 BY THE SHAH JAHAN IN MEMORY OF HIS WIFE.

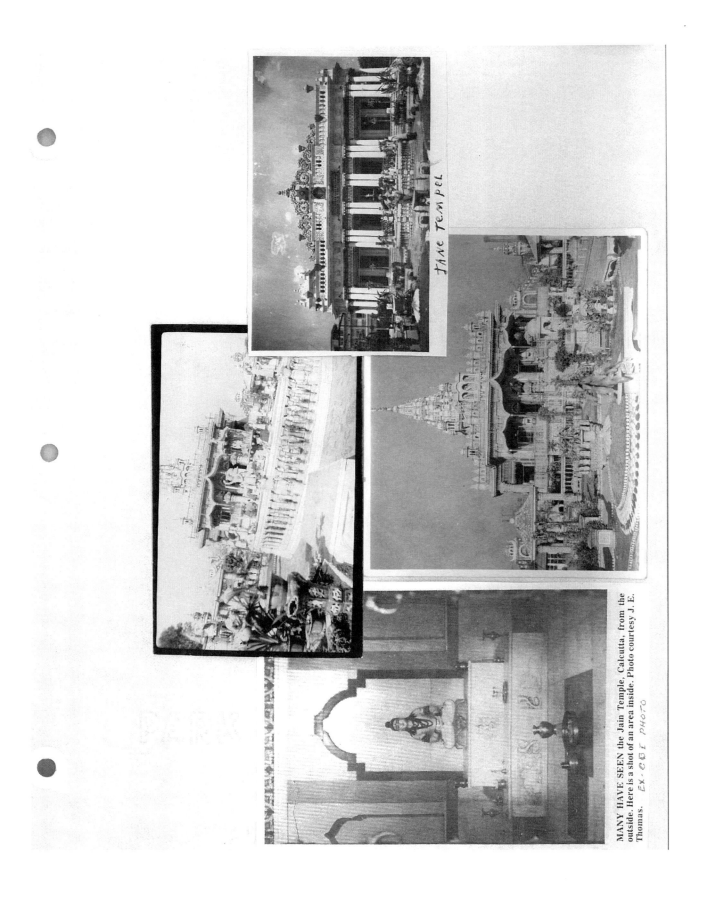

MANY HAVE SEEN the Jain Temple, Calcutta, from the outside. Here is a shot of an area inside. Photo courtesy J. E. Thomas. EX-CBI PHOTO

THIS COCONUT MARKET on Cornwallis street in Calcutta is an example of the haphazard way in which many bazaars were operated.

TEMPLE OF FERTILITY

We stayed at an Army Camp at Deem Dien about 12 miles from Calcutta. Oh what a strange people and places. The most famous place nearest American is called Firpos Drinks and Eats But will never compare to Minnesota. I also got into a fight with a British Sgt about 200 pounds. He first kicked me in the leg and I caught him with a left. So we wrestled a while and we hit the floor. I got a strangle hold on him around the neck and he kept yelling stop please. I said promise not to hit me and I'll let you go. Just then two British MP's walked in so we explained what happened and he took

we stayed at a Dum D im about Calcutta oh what places the most nearest american Drinks + Eats Back to Minnesota I also with a British Sgt first kicked me in Caught him we wrestled a while floor I got a strangle around the neck and yank stop please hit me I'll let you two British Majors explained what army camp at 12 miles from strange people famous place is called Firpos never will forget got in a fight about 200 lbs he the leg and I a left to me and we hit the angle hold on him he kept yelling I said promise not to go, just then walked in so we happened and he took

FIRPO'S RESTAURANT, on Calcutta's Chowringee Road, where thousands of CBIers dined. CBI pilgrims to the spot decades later found it had vanished. A bank had replaced it.

EX-CBI ROUNDUP

me into his party and we had a very interesting talk. So we saw some of the sights and on the 19th we started back at 3PM and that took 12 hours to come back. Oh I was tired and dirty. Came back and found things very upset at the Mess Hall. It took a few days to get things straightened out. So all is well today. We are waiting for the planes to come back from another mission. November 1, 1944 this morning I got up at 5 oclock got all dressed up warm and at 6:15 were high in the air in a B29. I spent until 12:45. Sure was a thrill. We went to northern Burma and

me into his party and we had a very interesting talk so we saw some of the sight's & on the 18th we started back at 3 P.M. and that took 1½ hrs to come back oh was I tired & dirty com- back and found things very upset at the mess hall. it took a few days to get it straightened out. so all is well today we are waiting for the planes to come back from another mission. Nov. 1 1944 this morning I got up at 5 oclock got all dressed warm and at 6:15 we were high in the air in a B 29 - I spent until 12:45 sure was a thrill we went to northern Burma and

20 MAN DITCHING PROCEDURE
TWENTY MAN DITCHING PROCEDURE
Hatched Areas Indicate Esc Hatches
Crew Members Perform Regular Ditching Duties
B-29 - HOODLUM - HOUSE II

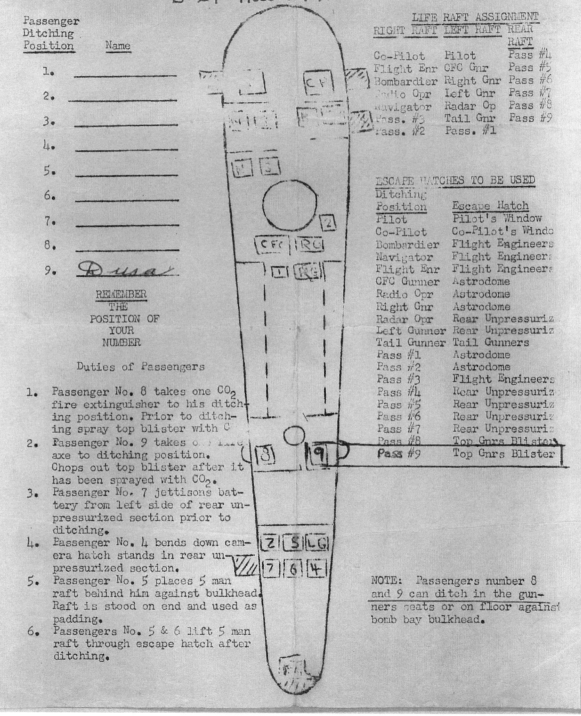

Passenger Ditching Position — Name

1. _____
2. _____
3. _____
4. _____
5. _____
6. _____
7. _____
8. _____
9. *Dusa*

REMEMBER THE POSITION OF YOUR NUMBER

LIFE RAFT ASSIGNMENT

RIGHT RAFT	LEFT RAFT	REAR RAFT
Co-Pilot	Pilot	Pass #4
Flight Enr	CFC Gnr	Pass #5
Bombardier	Right Gnr	Pass #6
Radio Opr	Left Gnr	Pass #7
Navigator	Radar Op	Pass #8
Pass. #3	Tail Gnr	Pass #9
Pass. #2	Pass. #1	

ESCAPE HATCHES TO BE USED

Ditching Position	Escape Hatch
Pilot	Pilot's Window
Co-Pilot	Co-Pilot's Windo
Bombardier	Flight Engineers
Navigator	Flight Engineer
Flight Enr	Flight Engineer
CFC Gunner	Astrodome
Radio Opr	Astrodome
Right Gnr	Astrodome
Radar Opr	Rear Unpressuriz
Left Gunner	Rear Unpressuriz
Tail Gunner	Tail Gunners
Pass #1	Astrodome
Pass #2	Astrodome
Pass #3	Flight Engineers
Pass #4	Rear Unpressuriz
Pass #5	Rear Unpressuriz
Pass #6	Rear Unpressuriz
Pass #7	Rear Unpressuriz
Pass #8	Top Gnrs Blister
Pass #9	Top Gnrs Blister

Duties of Passengers

1. Passenger No. 8 takes one CO_2 fire extinguisher to his ditching position. Prior to ditching spray top blister with C
2. Passenger No. 9 takes one fire axe to ditching position. Chops out top blister after it has been sprayed with CO_2.
3. Passenger No. 7 jettisons battery from left side of rear unpressurized section prior to ditching.
4. Passenger No. 4 bends down camera hatch stands in rear unpressurized section.
5. Passenger No. 5 places 5 man raft behind him against bulkhead. Raft is stood on end and used as padding.
6. Passengers No. 5 & 6 lift 5 man raft through escape hatch after ditching.

NOTE: Passengers number 8 and 9 can ditch in the gunners seats or on floor against bomb bay bulkhead.

dropped 13 bombs. I sure got a kick to watch how the radios worked. Today Nov 3. I am going to the hospital to have an x-ray taken for ulcers. I got out of the hospital. I had 14 x-rays taken and they claim it's a nervous stomach. So I asked to get out of the hospital. Things went along quite well. Well, then on thanksgiving we had a Big Dinner as our guest were Generals Upsilon, Rammey and LeMay. It was wonderful. Then I started to get Christmas packages from home and the pictures. On Dec 14th I got transferred to the Group HQ 462 Bomber Group. And on the 20th I chartered a plane to take me to Calcutta on business. Then we had a big Xmas Dinner.

> droped 13 Bombs I sure got a
> kick to watch how the radio
> worked, today 3 moved and tomorrow
> I am going to the hospital to have
> a tray taken. for ulcers. Nov 9th
> I got out of Hospital I had 14 xrays taken
> and they claim its a nervous stomach.
> so I asked to get out of the Hospital, things
> went along quite well. Then on thanks
> giving we had a Big Dinner our guest
> were General Upton Ramney, La May.
> it was wonderful. then I started to get
> Xmas packages from Home. and pictures
> on Dec 14th I got transfered to Gp Hq 462
> Bomb eye and on 20 the I chartered
> a plane to take me to Calcutta on
> Business, then we had a Big Xmas

General Curtis E. LeMay

1906-1990
B-29 Commander

General LeMay died October 1, 1990, at the March Field Hospital in Riverside, California. The general was struck by a sudden heart failure. Curtis LeMay was the combat commander of the 20th Air Force that included the India based 58th Bomb Wing. He served as Commander of the Strategic Air Command for nearly a decade, and also was Air Force Chief of Staff. He lived his later years in Long Beach, California.

General Curtis E. LeMay in the Marianas, 1945

NOVEMBER, 1990

EX-CBI ROUNDUP

Jinx Falkenburg in CBI

By Jinx Falkenburg

Copyright 1951
This story is a slight condensation of Chapter 8 of "Jinx — The Story of Jinx Falkenburg," published by Duell, Sloan and Pearce, New York, 1951. Copyright 1951, reprinted in Ex-CBI Roundup by special permission.

* * * * *

They told us that CBI would be hot.
They briefed us and prepared us and told us what to wear.

I believed them. So here I was flying over the Hump into China in bright red-to-the-knee socks, two turtleneck sweaters, a borrowed flight jacket, a pair of khaki shorts, and an oyxgen mask. It was freezing and this was the extent of my warm clothing. We all sat huddled on the floor, there were no seats on the plane, and four of the group, using parachutes as seats, played cards. I could feel myself off in my little corner getting dozier and dozier. This, I was sure, was the first sign of freezing to death, but it was such a wonderfully gentle sensation, I didn't have the strength to resist. We were flying 19,000 feet in the air somewhere between Chabua, India, and Kunming, China. We had already given a few shows in India and were now flying on to China "over the Hump" of the Himalayas, the graveyard of thousands of planes. You either flew at a freezing altitude in bad weather, as we were doing, or if the weather was good, flew just above the treetops. It wasn't much of a choice either way. Somebody was shaking me so vigorously my teeth shook.

I had forgotten to turn on my oxygen mask.

I wasn't tired or freezing. I had merely stopped breathing air!

Everybody thought it was very funny, or at least they laughed to release the tension.

But it really wasn't funny. It was a terribly rough trip.

Three hours of it.

"Oh, we're going to . . ." I didn't finish as we dove into an air pocket and a large mountain came looming up at us. Suddenly, out of nowhere, in the middle of mountain peaks, in the middle of nothing at all, there sat a tiny toylike shrine right on the top of one of the peaks. This, the pilot informed us, was a Japanese prison camp! It was a perfect day and I wondered how pretty it looked to the American boys down below.

This air route was used for everything. Everything from plane engines to beer cans had to come through here. I was astonished to think of the courage the boys had to have to make this flight day after day, but I supposed even that could become routine.

Suddenly, out from under a mountain, the Kunming field appeared. Our plane circled down in a tight spin, tighter and tighter, as I got sicker and sicker — and hotter and hotter. As we descended the temperature rose, rose, up and over my turtleneck sweater, until I was sure I was close to death by suffocation. We could hear the pilot of another plane calling on the inter-com and the intercom answering back:

"Four stars coming in, four stars, coming in . . ."

"I've got six stars in my ship," our pilot said.

"And I've got General Stilwell on my level."

The plane finally embraced the ground and out came a little jeep to meet Stilwell and his plane. Nobody expected us.

CBI had had notoriously bad luck with scheduled shows that didn't arrive, and,

IN PHOTO — JINX AND PAT O'BRIAN

156

TOP ROW - LEFT TO RIGHT
GEN. GODFREY, COL. KALBERER
GEN. RAMNEY, GEN. LE MAY
JAN. 15, 1945   LILY PONS -
ANDRE' KOSTALANTZ SHOW

PONS AND KOSTALANTZ ARRIVAL

Thanksgiving Supper.   11/30/44

- Punch Bowl — in center of table
- Each glass of cherry wine
- Chicken Soup w/Rice
- Croutons
- Canned Turkey
- Candied Sweet Potatoes
- Cream Gravy
- Cranberry Sauce
- Aspargus Buttered
- Escalloped Corn
- Cream Carrots
- Butter String Beans
- Cucumber + Onion Salad
- Mince Meat Pie
- Pumpking Pie
- Hot Rolls
- Ice Cream
- Candy
- Nutts
- Apples
- Bannas
- Oranges
- Coffee.

Hungry eh!
Come up and see me some time.
     Mess Sgt. Dusa.

Darjeeling Rest Camp and D. & H. Railroad

DARJEELING PHOTOS showing the city of Darjeeling, the D. & H. Railroad that was used to reach the rest camp, and Mt. Kanchanjunga. The buildings below the snow covered peak are part of the rest camp. Photos by Edward E. Sutton.

SGT. DUSA SPENT SEVERAL DAYS R AND R AFTER AN ILLNESS OF MALERIA

Most everyone was drunk. We had some pictures taken. Then New Years came along and we had a lot of big Generals. I had a few drinks after all the work was done. Then on the 7th of Jan we pulled a raid on Japan and we lost Lt Col Rousch a very nice fellow. And Dr. Lewis Max and Col Storey went home a good loss. Then on the 8th of Jan I talked to Col. Kalberer about my rating and told him its been six months since they promised me a rating and I asked him to see what he could do for me. And on Jan 10th the Special Order came out with my promotion to Staff. Sure happy. And on the 28th we closed up our little 80 man officer mess and on the 29th we opened

Dinner most every one had some pictures taken come along. and New Years, I had a few was done, then a raid on Japan an a very nice fellow. Col. Storry went home on the 8th of Jan about my rating now 6 mos since they and I asked him could do for me. and special order come permotion to Staff the 28 we closed officers mess, one

Jan 2-6 in Hospital with infection in nose was drunk. we then new years had a lot of big drinks after all work on 7th Jan we pulled we lost Lt Col Rousch and Dr Lewis Maj. a good lose. then I talked to Col Caleberer told him its been promised me a rating to see what he on Jan 10th the out with my sure Happy. and on your little 80 man 29th Jan we opened

OFFICERS' MESS
ICE CREAM - A RARE TREAT
MESS SGT. DUSA PROMOTED TO STAFF/SGT.

BELOW
COL. KALBERER
SGT. KOKOT

MAJ TRITES AND MAJ. THURSTING IN PHOTO ABOVE - PIARDOBA

CHRISTMAS INDIAN STYLE at the air base at Piardoba. Photo by Clarence Miller.

B-29 Base at Kharagpur

Japanese Bombs for Christmas

By Gene L. Whitt

Christmas night of 1944 we were given about an hours warning of a Japanese air raid. When the alarm went off we went into our slit trenches beside each tent. Up to that time, more often than not, the trenches had been used as latrines. After a very short time we vowed never to make such use again. After what seemed a very long wait, we began to see the ack-ack begin to fire in all directions. A 40mm pom-pom was about a hundred yards from us. It seemed to be firing in every direction into the starlit night but not at anything we could see. On one occasion I did see a plane as it cut through the stars but no one was firing at it.

Shortly after the firing ceased we could see fire down by the line (where the planes were). By then we were quite unhappy with the smell in the trenches so four of us took a small truck and headed for the fires. A barracks-like building was on fire. We were told that more planes were coming and that we should get the fire out as soon as possible. I took a hose and directed it where the flames seemed brightest. This happened to be right at the peak of the roof which was burning through. After about ten minutes, a fellow came around the building to urge me to aim the hose lower since I was getting the crews on the other side wet.

Just as we got the worst of the flames out, a soldier walked up to me carrying a 100 lb. bomb that had failed to go off. We debated what to do with it and decided to put it into a barrel and fill the barrel with water. This we did very carefully but I'm not sure to this day if we did the right thing. Afterwards the four of us went back to the tent area and told them where we had been. They didn't believe us until they smelled the smoke odor in our clothes.

The next day we found out that the planes had been Japanese twin engine bombers. They burned a C-87 or a B-24 used as a transport and the barracks. I don't know of any other damage. We were told that British Beaufighters had shot all the Japanese down before they could get back to Burma.

PARKER
NELSON, CHAP.
CONMEY ARC
OPERSENDIK
MR. TERRY ARC
DUANE
STAN T.R.
TECH REP.

MAJ. ELLERBE
FATHER STEVENS
BETTY
TEMPLE
ZALSKIE
ROMANE

CHRISTMAS
DECEMBER '44
CAPT. FLEMING
COL. NORMAN
CAPT. KLUG

COLONEL KALBERER CENTER OF PHOTO

NEW YEAR'S PARTY JANUARY 1945

M/S KOKOT, T/SGT DUSA LEFT AND SECOND TO LEFT

S/Sgt Dusa

RESTRICTED

HEADQUARTERS
462ND BOMBARDMENT GROUP
APO 220

10 January 1945

SPECIAL ORDERS)
:
NUMBER   8)

1. Under the provisions of AR 615-5 as amended and Memo 35-24 Hq XX BC dated 10 July 44 Sgt Martin Dusa 17 049 855 this Hq is promoted to the temp gr of S Sgt vice original vacancy.

RESTRICTED

SO 8 Hq 462nd Bomb Gp APO 220 dated 10 Jan 44 cont'd:

By order of Colonel KALBERER:

WILLIAM S. TRITES,
Major, Air Corps,
Adjutant.

OFFICIAL:

WILLIAM S. TRITES,
Major, Air Corps,
Adjutant.

Sgt. Martin Dusa, 20th Bomber Command, somewhere in India, was promoted to staff sergeant Jan. 14 and on the same date completed a year of overseas duty. S/Sgt. Dusa enlisted Feb. 2, 1942, and had two years training and service in the United States before leaving for overseas, where he has been stationed in Africa and India.

Insignia Chevrons Non-Commissioned officers

INSIGNIA CHEVRONS
NON-COMMISSIONED OFFICERS

COLONEL ALFRED F. KALBERER

Our commanding officer has all the characteristics and experience that qualify him for his position as the Number 1 Hellbird. He was part of the growing air age of the Twenties when, after giving up a medical career, he enrolled at the Army's Brooks and Kelly Flying Schools. Completing his training he joined Major Royce's famed First Pursuit Squadron flying Curtis Hawks. Leaving the army, Col. Kalberer embarked on an odyssey that saw him first conducting aerial advertising for General Tire Company and later flying with airlines all over the world. Just prior to Pearl Harbor, the colonel was flying for the Dutch Air lines which took him to all capitals of Europe and the Far East. On December 8th he rejoined the army and after completing a survey of all countries from Egypt to Australia, joined Colonel Halverson's B-24 Task Force on its way to China. This group was sidetracked in the Middle East, where it made an enviable record against the Italians and the Nazis. Back in the States after extensive Mediterranean activity, the colonel, refusing a Washington desk job, joined the B-29's for further combat activity in the war against Japan. Following the loss of Colonel Carmichael a few months after leaving the States, Colonel Kalberer has been our leader.

A tireless and energetic officer, he has led his group to an enviable position among combat units of the Army Air Forces. A fearless pilot, he is emphatically proud of the Hellbirds and their accomplishments.

our commanding officer

462nd Bomb Group Officers' Club, India

Officers' Mess - PIARDOBA, INDIA
Left to Right - RALPH RAVELLI

JAN. 30, 1945
NEW CONSOLIDATED
Officers' Mess

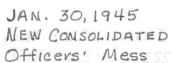

MANGELRIES
DOLLAR
RIVERA
SHANE

JANUARY 30, 1945
HELLBIRD HAVEN
OFFICERS' MESS

462nd BOMB GRP.
OFFICERS' MESS PERSONNEL
1944   INDIA

KNEELING
CPL. SHANE - CALIF.
PVT. RINGLER
CPL. RIVERA   P.A.
CPL. HEBERT   TENN.
SGT. JACKSON   MAHNOMEN, MN.
PVT. OWENS   MONTANA

BACK ROW
SGT. DUSA - MESS SGT. MN.
PVT. AMBIOSE
PVT. WILSON   KANSAS
PVT. ROSENBLUM   N.Y.
PVT. ZELAZO
CPL. HAHAN   SO. DAK.
CPL. LOGAN

MISSING FROM PHOTO
PVT. WEBSTER
PVT. McCAFFRAY
CPL. YOUNG

462ND BOMBARDMENT GROUP

HELLBIRD FLEDGLINGS

You have been proposed for membership in the Hellbird Fledglings, an association of young people interested in the Hellbird Group, and you have been accepted as a member. Your membership card and a Fledgling patch are being sent to you. The patch bears a replica of the insigne which appears on all B-29 aircraft assigned to the 462nd, or Hellbird Group.

As a member of the Fledglings there are certain facts you should know about the Hellbird Group:

1. It is one of the four original groups to fly and test the B-29 in combat. It took part in the first attack by land-based airplanes against the Japanese mainland.

2. In 9 months it flew a distance equal to 80 times around the World in attacking Japanese targets from the Group's India and China bases.

3. It took part in the longest day and longest night bombing missions ever flown.

4. It was the first Group to lay aerial mines from a B-29. It conducted the longest aerial mining operation on record.

5. On one of its missions it carried a greater weight of bombs for a greater distance than ever before carried by any aircraft.

6. It was the first Group to fly a B-29 completely around the world.

Your membership in the Hellbird Fledglings authorizes you to wear the Fledgling patch either on the left breast of your jacket or on the left sleeve 3/4 inch below the shoulder seam. As a member of the Fledglings you assume the obligation of conducting yourself in accordance with the traditions of the Hellbird Group.

For the Membership Committee:

Joseph R. Fawcett
JOSEPH R. FAWCETT,
Major, Air Corps,
Chairman.

Hellbird Fledglings
MEMBERSHIP CERTIFICATE
This certifies that **MARTIN LEE DUSA**
is a member of the Hellbird Fledglings and as such is entitled to wear the Fledgling patch bearing a replica of the insigne of the Hellbird Group.

Proposed by ....
Signed:
Alfred Kilburn
Col., A.C.

THE STORY of the Hellbirds is the story of the B-29 Superfort, its debut and development as the most efficient strategic weapon to be employed by any military organization in the world. The chapters of this history tell a story, not only of the lives, the travels and the activities of men drawn from the comfortable surroundings of civilian life into the turmoil of war, but also of the many problems solved by these men and of their untiring efforts to prove the Superfort the most powerful weapon of the American Armed Forces. The B-29 project, launched at a time when a Superfort was still a novelty and production plans were still being formed, saw complete and gratifying success in two simultaneous accomplishments . . . the "de-bugging" of the Superfort and the proving of its power "de-bugging of the SUPER FORT, AN THE and effectiveness as a combat weapon. At the same time AND AIR WHATS crews, both ground and air, were learning the whats, whys, ifs and hows of this new bomber, the bomber itself was participating in the first long range strikes against strategic targets in the Japanese home islands and in other areas of the Empire previously inaccessible to Allied aircraft.
EMPIRE

To accomplish these results Washington chose its men carefully. From all points of the globe, from every theater of war officers and men, veterans of every type of aerial combat and activity, were brought together to form the four Groups of the 58th Bombardment Wing of the XX Bomber Command, the first organization to be assigned B-29's for combat duty. From these parent Groups were later taken the cadres for newer organizations to form the Groups and Wings of the XXI Bomber Command, which the Hellbirds were to join after a year of intensive combat flying in India and China. But this will be covered later in our chapter on Tinian Island

The chapters comprising this short history of the Hellbirds depict the lives and travels of thousands of men from the date of their activation, through long days of training, the voyages IN INDIA to Asia, the year of combat in India and China, the travels to Tinian Island and their life and combat activities there, through the end of the war and those months spent "sweating out THE WAR AND THOSE MONTHS return to the States.

The oldest B-29's in the business are bombing from Tinian after an epic 3600-mile trek.

India Wing

The oldest B-29's in the business—not-so shiny veterans of sweltering, cooliebuilt China airbases and gruelling flights over the Hump, celebrated their first birthday in June by smashing at Honshu again and again from their new home on Tinian. The historic 58th Wing, which has bombed every Jap nerve-center from India to Tokyo, got a glittering birthday present in the form of Presidential Unit Citations for all four groups in the Wing. With their new ribbons, the old-time ground and air crews could look back on some big changes in the 12 months since their initial strike against Siam, including a great air-sea trek of 3600 miles—from India to the Marianas—which was completed without the loss of a man or a plane.

The vast migration of last February, March and April was conducted in such secrecy that the 58th's bombers had operated out of Tinian for more than a month before personnel were allowed to explain to their bewildered families why their APO had been changed from New York to San Francisco. Transporting an entire wing—from the bombers down to the last typewriter and orderly room cat—was no cinch, but the whole operation went off without a hitch and with practically no interruption in the outfit's main job of bombing the Japs.

Ground crews, administrative personnel and a few air crews left by water late in February. The Superforts continued their

ASSISTANT crew chief Cpl James W. Curtis looks over his B-29 which nearly crashed on takeoff from China. Scoreboard records telephone poles the bomber clipped off in very narrow escape.

THE CG, Brig Gen Roger M. Ramey, supervised 3600-mile hop from India to Marianas.

operations in India, turning out five combat and seven photographic missions in the following month. All maintenance work and engine changes were performed by the combat crews themselves during that month, under the direction of crew chiefs who stayed behind. The following month, the combat crews readied their aircraft for the long haul to Tinian, sweated out repeated weather postponements, and finally headed east.

Flight after flight, the big planes roared over the Hump from India to a secluded China base, gassed up and took off again for Tinian. They flew at night, separately, over carefully split-up routes, most of them heading between Formosa and the Philippines. Some flew over Jap-occupied Hongkong and reported being trailed by night fighters. A few had engine trouble and set down in the Philippines for short checkups. Only one had a serious mishap. The B-29 commanded by Lt Thomas F. Randle Jr., of Chico, Calif., headed out from a mountain base in China at night. The bomb bay doors flipped open at 300 feet on the takeoff. The airplane mushed and dropped almost to the ground, mowing down eight telephone poles and ripping her guts out nearly to the tail. Randle fought for control, but couldn't get enough height to clear a mountain at the end of the field. Luckily it was a moonlight night and he saw a valley to the left of the mountain. He banked into the cleft, and finally got the big bomber back to the ground. Under the crew chief's guidance, they patched her up, wired the bomb bays together and took off again two days later. Once at Tinian, they gave the ship a real overhaul. Then they painted eight telephone poles on her nose in addition to the camels signifying trips across the Hump and the bombs denoting missions.

Lt Randle's ship was the only one in the Wing which even came close to disaster on the long and hazardous trip. The rest of them pulled in to Tinian to find the Seabees had built roads, runways and hardstands, and that most of the ground personnel had just arrived. But the base was still far from completion. Ground and combat men alike buckled down to set up

(Continued on next page)

FOR THEIR FIRST MISSION. MUCH OF THE STRENGTH OF THE WING DERIVES FROM ITS COMMANDERS - MEN WHO WERE

India Wing (Cont'd)

handpicked by Gen Arnold to inaugurate the B-29 attacks. They are a colorful lot of old-timers, with an aggregate flying time that staggers the imagination.

Perhaps the most colorful of the lot is Col Alfred F. Kalberer, the CO of the Hellbird Group, whose motto: "With Malice Toward Some," is emblazoned on all of its bombers. Col Kalberer is an airlines veteran who looks like the movies' idea of a bomber pilot. That's not strange—he has written some movie scenarios for flying pictures in the early days.

Busy Colonel

"I was in Singapore in November of '41 when a friend of mine, an American-educated Jap flying a transport run in Burma, tipped me off that Japan would be at war with the U. S. by Christmas," he said. "So I grabbed the Clipper for home, taking off from Manila just as the Japs were attacking Pearl Harbor." Col Kalberer went into the Ferry Command and spent a month whipping up a book analyzing terrain, weather and other conditions from Egypt to India. Then he got involved in a highly secret affair in which three beat-up old B-24's were to make a token raid on Japan from bases in China. The bases were set up and everything was ready to go when the Doolittle raid was first planned, so his mission was called off. He went to Egypt then and joined up with Col Halverson's B-24 Task Force which carried out the first raid against the Ploesti oilfields. Of 13 Liberators in the flight, four returned to base, including his own. Then he took a small group of 24's against the Italian fleet off Sicily, setting fire to two battleships, diverting them from a British convoy, and chasing the fleet back to its harbor at Torrento, where it stayed for the rest of the war. His wildest project was a deal whereby he wanted to take a single B-24 in a night raid against the farmhouse which Intelligence had discovered Rommel was using as a headquarters near El Alamein. But the British called it off—it wasn't "sporting."

The Colonel now spends his spare time figuring out a way to sink Honshu and end the war. "A volcano expert told me once that if you could explode about 100 tons of bombs simultaneously in that active crater in Tokyo Bay, you could knock out the lava plug, let in the sea, and build up enough steam pressure to raise complete hell," he said. "I've been thinking it over. Now if we could get some of those 11-ton volcano bombs the British developed, and get a bunch of the boys in the Wing together, and fix the fusing just right...." He grinned dreamily. "Hot damn, that would really be something to watch, wouldn't it?"

*****

MacArthur and Stilwell

The photograph of Gen. of the Army Douglas MacArthur, left and four-star Gen. Joseph W. Stilwell was taken in 1945 outside MacArthur's HQ in Manila shortly before Stilwell was named to command of the Tenth Army. It is printed here by courtesy of Col. Paul L. Jones, an aide to Gen. Stilwell during the CBI days and during most of the general's World War II career.

*****

your commanding officer...

COL. ALFRED F. KALBERER

Col. Kalberer can proudly boast that he was a participant in the growing air age of the Twenties.

It was at this time that he gave up a medical career to enroll at Brooks and Kelly Flying school.

Upon completion of this training he joined Major Royce's famed First Pursuit Squadron, flying the Curtiss Hawk which had a top speed of 160 mph.

HEADQUARTERS
462ND BOMBARDMENT GROUP
APO 183

You are now a Hellbird--a member of the 462nd Bombardment Group. We selected this name many months ago in India after we realized the destructive potentialities of the B-29 by actual observation of results of early attacks. Today even the Japanese are of the same mind; they call us "Jigoku No Tori"--Birds of Hell!

You belong to a hard working, efficient air unit with a fine combat record and high morale. One of the four original B-29 Groups, we have been activated since July of 1943 and in combat since June, 1944. This booklet will orient you on our past and present history; one we are proud of since it is also a part of what is perhaps the greatest experiment the world has ever seen--- the attempted destruction of a nation by use of air power alone. Indications are that our efforts may meet with success, since the B-29 has proven to be not only the first true strategic bomber but capable of inspiring such fear in the hearts of the Japanese people that their will to fight, in spite of inborn fanaticism, is rapidly deteriorating.

By putting forth not just a fair effort--but your very best effort!--we can collectively save the lives of thousands of ground troops and shorten this war by at least a year. You will also have the satisfaction of knowing that you helped air power to cut its teeth and put it in a position to eat solid food.

If Japan capitulates without invasion, the tremendous outlay of effort, skill and money the B-29 program has cost will be vindicated.

So pitch in and help!

Alfred F. Kalberer
ALFRED F. KALBERER,
Colonel, Air Corps,
Commanding.

In India Many Had the 8 p.m.

Basha Snacks

By Dwight O. King

Now we're not talking about the guys moving daily through the Burma jungles. But, in the bashas a common practice was to bring out snacks and beer in the evening. Most packages sent from the States by friends and relatives contained "something for the boys to eat."

So, about 8 p.m. or so, someone would bring out his "goodies" sent from home. A wide variety of snacks would mysteriously appear out of foot lockers up and down the line. What we ate in those days would surely today send us poste haste to the medicine cabinet.

What were these gastronomical delicacies? Well, it seemed everyone had some kind of crackers. We had the hard kind and the kind that crumbled during transit. Rye, Wheat, Soda, Buttermilk; all of these at one time or another appeared on an old table, on a bunk, or sometimes on a blanket spread on the floor.

And we had cheese! Cheeses of all types came out to compliment the crackers. I recall that one of our guys was fond of Limburger. When he contributed to the "feast", some quickly left the party.

I guess there must have been a plethora of these in the States, for I have never seen so many contribute "Vienna Sausages." Before going overseas, I didn't know what one of these was. I soon found out. I could best describe them as a soggy and not particularly tasty small hot dog.

Candies and cookies were plentiful. Aunt Julia's favorite recipe arrived from Peoria in five pound boxes. Pickles, cucumbers, pigs knuckles, and other choice items very often were offered up.

It was in India that I first ventured to try "Red Hot Peppers" from Louisiana. One of our guys insisted that

everyone try them as they were the greatest. Run quick to the water jug!

Which brings us to the beer. We did have some beer which was highly coveted by all. I don't know why because it was usually hot out of the can. The variety of brands we got was amazing! Stateside breweries that hadn't operated in years began turning out the worst beer brewed in the 20th Century. I recall one brand titled "Fort Pitt." It was really the pits! We called it something else! (Sorry if this offends our Pennsylvania folks.)

Well, after we gorged ourselves on these and other delicious items, the spreads would disappear as quickly as they appeared to reign another evening.

Can't knock these sessions too much as they were a way to establish pleasant sociability among the troops. We did enjoy them. That's the way we passed some evenings in the CBI. Remember?

the consolidated officers mess which we feed 465 officers. Ralph was in charge but just in title and I was assistant. Things were rough the first few days but it all came out well. We were to get 100 Rupees extra a month for working there so on Feb 15th we got 50 rupees and I was relieved of duty to be shipped out. But I still worked there. So on the night of Feb 22nd at 9 oclock we 35 HQ boys packed out bags, loaded them on trucks, then on the train, and at 1 oclock we pulled out, about 1000 of us. We reached Calcutta at 8:30 23 Feb then carried our A and B bags to a cruise boat and went down stream. What should be anchored near but a large American boat, a Big one. The name USS Gen McCray. There are 4000 of us on board and talk about crowded. Its almost impossible to get around. Today is Monday 26th we are still on ship in port. We are to leave tomorrow, the 27th my birthday what a gloomy way to spend a birthday, same as last year on a boat. This ship is a large new all steel ship only 6 months old. We are way down in he hole 5P and no air, Hot and stuffy. March 1st we pulled out from Calcutta. On March 5 we crossed the equator. Oh talk about hot and sunburn. Boy I peeled all my skin. On the 7th of March they had an initiation for the troops.

the Consolated officers mess which we felt
465 officers Ralph was in charge. But
Just in title and I was assestent
things were rough the first few days
But it all Came out well. we were
to get 100 Ruppes extra a month for
working ther, so. on Feb 15, we
got 50 R₃ and I was relieved of
Duty to be shiped out. But I still
worked ther, So on the night of the
22nd of Feb at 9oclock we 35 HQ Boys raped
our bags loaded them on trucks. At one
the train, at one oclock we pulled out
about 1000 of us. we reached Calcutta at 8ᴼ
23. Feb. then carried our A & B Bags to a
Crause boat and went down stream
what should be anchored near

but a large american Boat a Big one. the
nam U.S.S. Gen. McCray there are 4000 of us
on board. and talk about crouded its
almost impossible to get around. today is
monday 26th we are still on ship in
port. we are to leave tomarrow. 28 on
my Birthday what a gloomy way to
spend a birthday some as last year. on a
boat. this ship is a large new all
steel ship only 6 mo old we are way down
in the hole 5D. and no air Hot &
stuffy. March 1st we pulled out
from Calcutta, on March 5th we
crossed the equator oh talk about and
sun burnt boy I sealed all of my
skin on thy 5th March they
had a anstalation for the troops
initiation

Eleven months - Eleven days in INDIA

MARCH 20, 1944   ARRIVED AT BOMBAY
MARCH 25,   ARRIVED AT KHARAGPUR
MAY 7,   ARRIVED AT PIARDOBA
    60 mi. from KHARAGPUR
    137 mi. from CALCUTTA
FEB. 22, 1945   DEPARTED PIARDOBA
FEB. 23,   ARRIVED AT CALCUTTA
MARCH 1, 1945   DEPARTED CALCUTTA ON
    TROOP SHIP U.S.S. GEN. McRAE

GENERAL J. H. McRAE

Length, overall 522' 10"	Gross tons 13,000	Propulsion Turbine
Beam 71' 6"	Speed (knots) 17	Passengers 3,054
Draft 24' 0"	Radius (miles) 15,000	Cargo (cu. ft.) 32,480

Built in 1944 by Kaiser Co., Inc., Richmond, Calif.

THIS C4 type vessel was named in honor of Major General James Henry McRae, Class of 1886, U. S. Military Academy, who served in various campaigns of the Spanish-American War (in Cuba and the Philippines) and in the St. Mihiel and Argonne operations of World War I. General McRae was later Assistant Chief of Staff.

Following construction, the GENERAL J. H. McRAE went to Seattle from where she sailed on 21 September 1944 for Honolulu. She returned to San Francisco in early October and made another trip to Honolulu via Puget Sound. On 20 November the ship departed from San Francisco for Finschhafen and Oro Bay. On 11 January 1945 the vessel left Los Angeles for a four months cruise to the Southwest Pacific and beyond. Ports visited include in the order named: Melbourne, Bombay, Melbourne, Townsville, Manus, Ulithi, Tinian, Saipan, Manus, Townsville, Biak, Morotai and Leyte. This voyage, terminated at San Francisco on 30 May, ended her Pacific Ocean service for the time being.

The GENERAL McRAE transited the Panama Canal in late June and proceeded to Le Havre, Cherbourg and Marseilles. Returning in late August to Hampton Roads, the ship sailed, via Port Said, for Karachi, India, and came back to New York in mid-October. The McRAE left New York on 26 October for a voyage, via the Suez Canal to Khorramshahr (Iran) and Karachi (India). Return to New York was on Christmas Eve 1945.

On 27 February 1946, the vessel was transferred to the Army and alterations were accomplished by Atlantic Basin Iron Works at New York between 19 March and 27 May to fit the ship for peacetime operation by the War Department.

101

TROOP SHIPS OF W WAR II
BY
RONALD W. CHARLES
PUBLISHED 1947

S-N-A-I-L-G-R-A-M   No. 12345678

FLASH:
Our communication system has intercepted a seaweed signal from the domain of Neptunus Rex, in the equatorial waters of the South Pacific. In part this snailgram read:

"DEAR DAVY, IT HAS COME TO MY ATTENTION THAT THE GOOD SHIP GENERAL J.H. McRAE WILL ENTER MY DOMAIN FROM THE NORTH SOMETIME IN THE NEAR FUTURE, LOADED WITH ONE OF THE SCUMMIEST COLLECTIONS OF POLLIWOGS, WORMS, TADPOLES, NEWTS, AND ALL OTHER MANNER OF SLIMY CRAWLING THINGS FROM THE MUD RIMMED LAND-LOCKED FRESH-WATER MARSHES, THAT EVER SET A CRUMMY SAIL ON OUR CLEAN BLUE SALT-WATER EMPIRE. THEY ARE GUIDED BY A NUMBER OF STALWART, LOYAL SUBJECTS; STURDY BRAVE MEN WHO WILL BE REWARDED ON THE DAY OF TRIUMPHAL ENTRY. HOWEVER, THERE ARE THOSE WHO CLAIM TO BE EXALTED SHELL-BACKS BUT ARE IN REALITY LOWLY POLLIWOGS, MAKING IT NECESSARY FOR ALL ALLEGED SHELLBACKS TO PRESENT THEIR CREDENTIALS PRIOR TO 1600 ON THIS DAY. PLEASE SEE THAT THIS IS DONE DAVEY . . . .

FURTHER, THERE HAS BEEN ORDERED SUPPLIED YOU IMMEDIATELY IN ACCORDANCE WITH THE NECESSITIES OF THE CASE, ONE HUNDRED BARRELS OF COAL TAR, TWENTY-FIVE GALLONS OF VARNISH, ONE TEN POUND POUCH OF SULPHUR, TWO HUNDRED SETS OF ... (TWENTY-FOUR INCHES), FIFTEEN SE... KNIVES, SIX MEAT CLEAVERS AND O... IRONS. THESE SUPPLIES TOGETHER ... WILL COMPLETE YOUR REQUIREMENTS ... WILL SEE THAT ALL IS IN READINE... ARRIVAL OF MYSELF AND STAFF ON ... POLICEMEN'S CLUBS MUST CONFORM ... WILL TAKE CARE EACH NIGHT TO SE... LOOSE FOR EXERCISE. YOU WILL A... SUCH CREATURES AS YOU DEEM TO B... CAUSE.

> **Domain of Neptunus Rex**
> RULER OF THE RAGING MAIN
> TO ALL TRUSTED SHELLBACKS OF THE SEVEN SEAS and all Living Things of the Sea:
> GREETINGS: Know ye that on this 5th day of March 19 45 in Latitude 00000 and Longitude 82°55' there appeared within Our Royal Domain the U.S.S. GENERAL J.H. McRAE
> BE IT REMEMBERED that the said Vessel, Officers, Crew and Passengers thereof have been inspected and passed on by Myself and My Royal Court. And Be It Known: By all ye Sailors, Marines, Soldiers, and others who may be honored by his presence that
> S/Sgt. Martin Dusa 7049855
> having been found worthy to be numbered as one of our Trusty Shellbacks has been duly initiated into the SOLEMN MYSTERIES OF THE ANCIENT ORDER OF THE DEEP.
> Davey Jones   Neptunus Rex
> His Majesty's Scribe   by his Servant

At 1830 - 5 March 1945, the Good Ship GENERAL J.H. McRAE was hailed and told to lay-to by Davy Jones. The Commanding Officer of the U.S.S. GENERAL J.H. McRAE was presented with the following:

"Commanding Officer,
"U.S.S. GENERAL J.H. McRAE
"Greetings:

"It has been brought to my attention, through my trusty Shellbacks; that the GENERAL J.H. McRAE, manned by a crew of loyal shellbacks, is loaded to the scuppers with polliwogs of the lowest order, who have not yet acknowledged the sovereignty of the Ruler of the Deep, and who have transgressed on my Domain and thereby incurred my Royal Displeasure.

"Be it known that I; Neptunus Rex, Supreme Ruler of all mermaids, sharks, squids, crabs, whales, denizons of the deep, and all living things of the sea, will, with my Royal Court, meet in full session on board your offending ship at 0800 tomorrow morning, to examine into the fitness of all land-lubbers to be taken into the Citizenship of the Deep and to hear their defense on the various and sundry charges that have been placed against them.

Some cut their hair in all shapes and put flowers on. Then greased and dumped into a tub of water. And then paddled their seats. I missed the affair as I was sort of under the weather with a patch on my eye and a boil on my head. Today the 12th we fired all the guns on the ship. The target was a balloon they let go and shot at as a target. There is another ship with us. We are LIRP shipment No # 5050. 57001-VX. And the other ship was D U V A. Today is March 17, 1945 At 6 AM this morning we spotted land and sailed into the harbor all day. And at 5:45 tonight we docked the ship. Not a soldier can get off for any reason. Sailors and Marines got shore leave but we have to stay on board. We are to stay here for seven days. The city lays behind us; we can't see any of it at all except lights. Just one year ago today we were nearing Bombay. I also got my stripes back. Well that's all I can say for now except that everyone is very disappointed because we can't get off. March 21st Wed. We got a pass for 12 hours to visit Melbourne.

cut of there hair and put flowers and then dumped and then really seats. I missed I was sort of with a patch a Boil on my 12th we fired the ship the balloon they use as a target ship with us shipment no # and the outher D.4.A. today is Sat at 6 AM this morning

in all shapes on them & grease into tub of water paddles over the why affair as under the weather on my Eye and head. Today the all the Guns on target was a go. and shot at there is another we are LIRP 5050. 57001-YX. ship load was March 17th 45 ning we spoted

land and sailed all day. and we docked tied soldier can get sailors & Marines But we have to we are to stay the city lays cant see any except lights. a go today we Bombay and I boys. well thats for now except is very disapointed cant get off a pass for 12 hrs

in the Harbor at 5.45 tonight ship and not a off for any reason got short leave stay on board here for 7 days. behind us we of it at all. Just one year were nearing also got my stripe all I can say that every one because me March 21st Wed- we got to visit Melbourne

```
                    HEADQUARTERS
         OFFICE OF THE ARMY TRANSPORTATION OFFICER
              USS GENERAL J. H. McRAE (AP - 149)

                                            15 March 1945
MEMORANDUM )
             :
NUMBER   15 )

              SHORE LEAVE AND LIBERTY IN MELBOURNE

     1. For the information and guidance of all Troops and
Passengers paragraph 2 of Melbourne File "Information for U. S.
Naval Vessels Entering Port" is quoted below:

     "2. AN AREA GENERAL ORDER DIRECTS THAT TROOPS (OFF-
ICERS AND MEN) OR THROUGH PASSENGERS, REGARDLESS OF NATIONAL-
ITY OR STATUS, SHALL NOT BE ALLOWED ASHORE IN MELBOURNE.

     Commanding Officers of transports are requested to
see that this GHQ directive is strictly enforced, and that
there are no unauthorized messages or telephone calls between
ship and shore by troops or passengers."

     2. Troops are forbidden to communicate, while in
Melbourne, with anyone not now embarked in this vessel, either
verbally, by phone, or by message.

              By order of the Army Transportation Officer:

                                        W. W. NEWSOM
                                        Captain, AC,
                                        Adjutant.
```

AUSSIE UNIFORM

Route followed in transfer from Piardoba, India to Tinian Island aboard troopship U.S.S. General J. H. McRae — 38 days

- Calcutta, India — March 1, 1945
- March 5, 1945 — Equator — Neptune Rex Ceremony
- The Pacific Ocean
- March 12, 1945 — Gun Drill Aboard Ship
- March 17, Spotted Land
- Melbourne — March 21, 12-hour pass
- Brisbane — March 26
- Townsville — March 26
- Madang — March 31
- Admiralty Island — April 1st, Easter Sunday
- New Guinea
- Australia
- Caroline Is. — April 5
- Marianas Islands: Saipan, Tinian — April 7, Guam

Then on the 23rd Friday we left Melbourne. We lost about 30 troops that missed the ship. Then on the 26th we picked up a pilot at Brisbane. We are headed for Townsville, Australia. We reached Townsville on Friday the 26th we pulled into the harbor at 5:30 PM. We picked up 385 Australian soldiers. I met Bill, a nice fellow and master of ceremonies aboard ship. Then on Wed the 28th we reached New Guinea. Then on Sat the 31st we pulled into Maddong New Guinea and unloaded our 385 troops and pulled out right away. Today April 1 Easter Sunday. We are in sight of the Admiralty Islands. I have been in charge of the mess hall feeding all the troops and sailors for 10 days then my eye went bad. So I got relief. We pulled into harbor at 12:30 Easter Sunday and anchored out to refuel and take on water. We picked up 30 sailors who had their ship sunk and we are taking them to Guam. On April 2nd Monday we set sail again

then on the left Meborne. that missed the The 26 the we piott at Bris headed for we reached Friday 26. we and at 5:30 PM australian soldiers a new fellow cer monbes aboard Wed 28 we then on Sat into Maddong and unloaded and pulled out

23rd Fri we we lost 30 troops ship. then on piped up a bone we are townsville austraily tounsvill pulled into Harbor picked up 385 kro I met Bill a master of ship. Then on reched New Ginnie 31st we pulled New Ginnie our 385 troops right away

today April 1st we are in admerlety admerlaties I have been the mess all troop & s then my bad. 16 I we pulled into sunday. and to refuel & picked up 30 where ship was taking them on April 2nd sail again

Easter Sunday. sight of the Ilands. in charge of hall feeding sailors for 10 day we went got relief Harbor at 12:30 Easter anchored out take on water sailors who had and we are to Guam. and monday we set nearing our for our destination Saipan. Today Wed April 4, 1945 we are in sight of the Caroline Islands, the most beautiful sight I have ever seen – ships in every direction – just as far as the eye can see. We anchored at 7:30 PM in the midst of the ships. Thursday the 5th we pulled out at 11:35 AM all alone with one escort. We are still heading for Guam. No body can ever sleep on deck, everyone on the ship hates the Captain of the ship. Today April 7 Saturday we got to Tinian at noon. We climbed down the side of the ship on ropes into a Invasion Barge, then about two miles to shore. Oh yes, what a sight. Not a thing here but a lot of Japs in the caves and all dug in the coral in the caves. Yesterday they killed 27 and everyone has to carry his gun. We are on a high hill. I got my shelter half and some straw and made a bed and nothing to eat but K rations. Today April 8 Sunday. I had a fairly good nights rest. We are located facing west and can see the ocean all around. Today is Thurs the

destination
Wed april 4, 1945
sight of the
the most beautiful
have ever seen
direction just
eye can see
at 7:30 PM in
ships and
pulled out at 1135
with one
self heading
body can _____
every one on
Caption of the
7th Sat we
at noon we

the side of the
into a invasion
town mily
yes, what a
thing here
Japs in Caves
the Coral
they killed 27
to carry his gun
hill. so I got
and some straw
and nothing to
today april 8,
fairly good
are located
and can see
all around.

Sipan, today
we are in
Carolines Islands
utiful sight
ship in every
as far as the
we anchored
the midst of
rsday the 5 of we
AM all alone
Escort we are
for Guam. no
sleep on Deck
the ship Hates the
ship. today april
got to tianian
climbed down

ship on ropes
Barge then about
to shore. oh!
sight not a
but a lot of
and all dug in
in caves yesterd
and Every on ship
we are on a high
my shelter half
and made a bed
ect But K Rations
Sunday I had a
night rest we
faceing West
the ocean
today is thur the

tinian ..

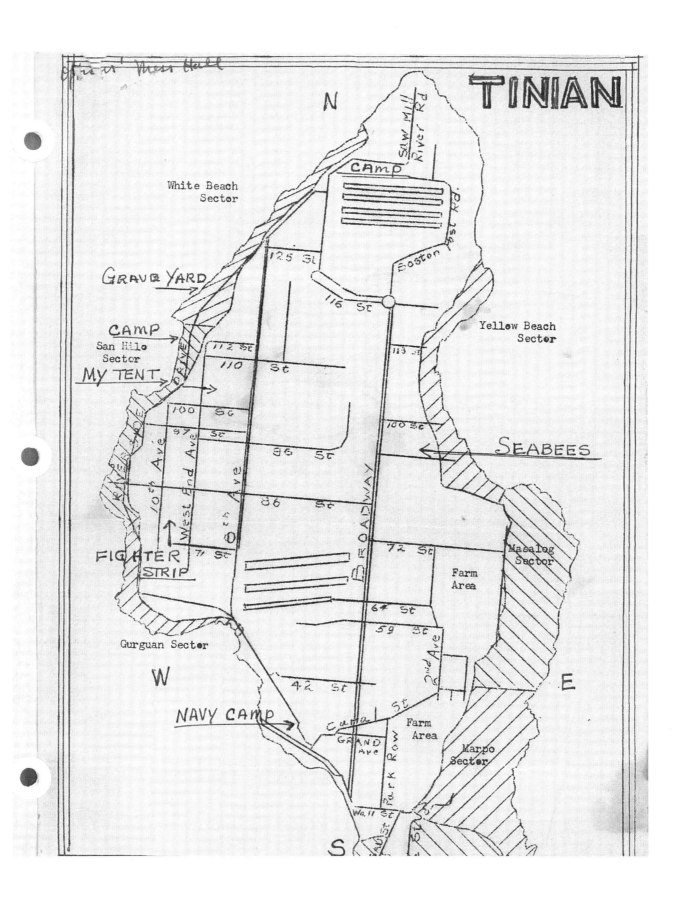

18th of April. A lot of things have already happened since we have been here. We got some big tents; we had to cut all the sugar cane in the field first and then put up our tents. It rains most every day. We had only one mail call thus far. On the 13 of April we got the news of FDR dying. We were all stunned. We have a lot of SEABEE's here doing all the building. They put up a big mess hall for us, a consolidated one where we feed 1385 troops. 768, 769, 770 and the Group HQ and 13 Photo. As yet we are waiting for our

18 of april a lot of things have already happened since we have been here, we got in some big tents we had to cut all the sugar cone in the field first then put up our tents, it rains most each day we had only on mail call thus far and on the 13th april we got the news of FDR dying were all stuned, the have a lot of sea Bees here doing all the building so they put up a big mess hall for us a Consolated one, where we feed 1385 troops. 768, 769, 770 and P. Hq & 13 photo so yet we are waiting for our

Do You Remember Where You Were On . . .

April 12, 1945?

Four of crew 22, 792nd Squadron, 468th Bomb Group, were at the B-29 base at Kharagpur, India. These four guys were relaxing about an hour before sundown on the porch outside their thatched roof basha. Cans of beer were being quaffed down as these four languished in the wicker chairs. It had been about an hour since they had returned from the mess hall where they had eaten their dinner which featured the usual Spam. A "sacred cow" strolled by and chewed a small chunk of greenery from the scraggly bush that grew just outside the basha front door. And, presently an Indian peanut vendor came by with his bag of nuts over his shoulder. A few annas were exchanged and peanuts became part of the beer party. The day had been a day like many others, for crew 22 had enjoyed a day relaxing with no mission to fly.

The levity of the hour was suddenly shattered when the paperboy arrived with the day's "Statesman" newspaper. The bold headline read, "Roosevelt Dead." It couldn't be! But, there it was! Beer cans were randomly placed on the floor of the cement porch and peanuts were devoured with a sudden gulp. The four Americans searched each others faces with a combination of sorrow and non belief.

The foursome would later learn that the President had gone to Warm Springs, Georgia, on March 29th. April 12th had begun for him as usual. He read newspapers and mail that had been flown from Washington. He planned to attend a barbecue in the afternoon. Before the barbecue, Roosevelt was working at his desk while an artist, Mrs. Elizabeth Schoumatoff, painted his portrait. Suddenly he fell over in his chair. "I have a terrific headache," he whispered. These were Roosevelt's last words. He died a few hours later of a cerebral hemorrhage.

Millions of people in all parts of the world would mourn his passing. That was April 12, 1945. Crew 22 remembers. Where were you in the CBI, and do you remember that day?

Dwight O. King

32nd President of the United States, 1933-1945

ROOSEVELT, *ROH zeh velt.* **FRANKLIN DELANO,** *DEL ah noh* (1882-1945), held the office of President longer than any other man. In spite of a strong tradition that no President should serve more than two terms, Roosevelt's countrymen chose him four times. Some persons who voted for Roosevelt in 1944 had been only nine years old when he was first elected.

President Roosevelt led the United States through the worst depression, as well as the greatest war, in the country's history. Authorities still disagree as to the wisdom of Roosevelt's measures for dealing with the depression. There are also differing views on whether he recognized the seriousness of the Soviet threat to world security, in his conferences with other heads of state near the end of World War II. But there is general agreement that he was a dynamic war leader.

Roosevelt had his greatest following among small-wage earners. Many business and professional persons opposed his policies. A few persons hated him with a strong, personal hatred. Probably no other President since Abraham Lincoln has aroused such deep devotion or such intense bitterness.

Roosevelt's place in history is secure, not only because of the stirring times through which he served, but also because of his own actions as President, debatable though they may be. Roosevelt brought to the office of President a new concept of the duties of the Federal Government. He held that the Government was a means through which the people might properly seek to better their conditions. He declared that a third of the nation was "ill-fed, ill-clothed, and ill-housed," and that it was the duty of the Government to raise their living standards. During his Presidency, such measures as unemployment compensation and social security became part of American life. The United States Government exercised greater control over business, both large and small, than ever before in history. It spent billions of dollars on poor relief and on public works to "prime the pump" of national business activity. Roosevelt created in the minds of millions an image of himself as the understanding friend and protector of the common people.

Critics of his policies argued that Roosevelt centered too much power in the Federal Government, and took from the states functions which were rightfully theirs under the Constitution. A number of court decisions supported this view. Many businessmen and others regarded the strict controls over business as harmful to the operation of the free-enterprise system. Another frequent criticism of Roosevelt's policies was that he exaggerated the possibilities of government help to the people, since in the long run it must be the people who pay for such help through taxation.

Roosevelt reached the height of his great popularity at the beginning of his second term. After that, group after group fell away from him. Many of the bankers, the businessmen, the professional groups, and at last even the farmers decided that they could no longer support his policies.

But Roosevelt was still popular with one group which could easily outvote all others. This group was made up of the people who worked for wages. Many unorganized as well as organized workers were devoted to Roosevelt. In every large industrial city, he received huge majorities of votes at each election. Workers felt that they had found in Roosevelt a President whose acts showed that he cared about their welfare, even though they did not always agree with him.

As a person, Franklin Roosevelt was colorful and exciting. Publishers might oppose his views, but he was always "good copy" to the reporters and columnists of the working press. The President's bitterest opponents felt and recognized his charm. Friends and advisers often regretted his strong personal loyalties and his un-

7020

planes and combat crews to come in from India which should be any day now. We have a Tech Sgt in charge of the whole mess. I am Mess Sgt of the 769; its all temporary until they build an officers mess then I will move over there and take over. Where I am sitting facing directly west on a high hill you can see the ocean south and north and west. Oh its cool. But at night we don't dare go out of the tents as the Japs are right below us still in the caves. They turn on the big search lights on the caves at night so if some come out the guards can see them. There are a lot of Marines here guarding us and the stockade is full of Japs. Korean civilians are laborers here; they work on the island for us under guard. This island is 13 miles long and 7 miles wide. It is the biggest runway in the world. Four B29's can take off at the same time and each two minutes they take off. The fighter planes are overhead day and night and big ships out at sea; we can see them so plain from here. We are building, cleaning, improving and trying to make things as comfy as possible.

planes & Combat from India, any day now.

Sgt in Charge I am mess Sgt of only temporary a officer's mess over there & tap sitting facing the high hill ocean South & its Cool. But at dare go out of the Japs are hight in Caves they lights on the so if some Come can see them of Merians here the stockade is Korian civilian they work on the under Geuard miles long and the bigest run world 4 B 29's the same time they tape off. planes are over and the big we can see them here. we are Improving and things as comfy.

crews to come in which should be we have a teck of the whole mess the 769, its all until they build then I will move over. where I am directly west on you can see the north. & West. oh night we don't tent as the below us still turn on big serch Caves at night cat the Gaurds there are a lot Gaurding us and full of Japs + Jap laborer's here Island for us this Island is 13 7 wide. it is away in the Can tape of at and each 2 minuits and the fighter head day & night ship ant at sea m so plain from Building Cleaning trying to make as possiable

Comin' IN......

Officers' Mess Hall

HEADQUARTERS ISLAND COMMAND
APO #247 - c/o Postmaster
San Francisco, California

TINIAN

2 5093

384.4

AG-JJH/sp
19 July 1945

SUBJECT: Restricted Areas.

TO: Commanding Officers, All Units.

ATTENTION ** IMPORTANT ** ATTENTION ** IMPORTANT

1. Re-read Memorandum No. 45, Headquarters Island Command, APO 247, dated 15 June 1945, and take positive action in bringing these instructions to the attention of all personnel.

2. Armed patrols of the 147th Infantry have been in physical contact with small bands of Japanese military on both the east and west shores of the island during the past several days. There has been some small arms firing. Unauthorized persons, members of the Island Garrison, have been found in restricted areas. This is not only in direct violation of recently published instructions, but is exceedingly hazardous for the personnel involved. Our patrols will continue to operate for an indefinite period and all unauthorized persons must remain away from the restricted areas until the security map is republished.

UNAUTHORIZED PERSONNEL MUST STAY OUT OF RESTRICTED AREAS. EXTRA MAPS CAN BE MADE AVAILABLE AT HEADQUARTERS ISLAND COMMAND FOR PUBLICATION ON ANY BULLETIN BOARD.

Frederick V. H. Kimble

FREDERICK V. H. KIMBLE
Brigadier General, USA
Commanding

DISTRIBUTION: "A"

NOTE: THE JAPS ARE WEARING U.S. UNIFORMS. THEREFORE, UNIFORMS ARE NO PROTECTION.

KEEP OUT OF RESTRICTED AREAS

John A. Labeur Capt AC Security Officer

In the world today there are many strange happenings such that a few years ago people would have dreamed as being impossible or with the most optomistic mind, improbable. War is such an event as brings on many of these strange happenings. Yet with all that is going on in this world today people are overlooking one of the strangest phenomena of life itself. Never in the history of the world has life, the most precious of all our possessions been so cheap or ravaged to such an extent as it is today. Never has the human race seen such wholesale slaughter and mass destruction as it is seeing today. Yet by some innermost hope, by unprecedented tenacity and will, people all over the world are hanging on to life when all hope has vanished. What is this will to live when strength is gone. What is this hope that shines in their eyes at undisclosed moments. Medical science would probably explain it is flesh and blood in such degrees and proportions as to conceive a human body. That is all well and good. But it does not explain the fierceness with which these people rise again and again. What is it that keeps them going when all is gone that they once knew as being decent and clean when that which once made hearts sing has vanished. Can it be that in their minds they still cling to the thoughts that hope is not lost as long as life remains in the body. It may be but I think that one big contributing factor still remains untouched upon. The spirit of God which all men have in their hearts and souls, that is the thing which makes them such as they are. The desire to see fair play, the unknown quality that holds life and hope in the body is not to be denied. Our Lord died that we might live on and on to believe in and teach his principles. In us he imbedded the desire to live on for what we believe to be right, as he would have taught us to believe. We are living examples of what he belived in; his doctrines of holiness, happiness, peace and life. He left for us to carry on. That is why we fight on when hope seems to be gone: that is why we fight on for things as they used to be. That is why we will once again hear the joyfull patter of childrens feet or see their happy shadows as they trudge off to school or to the corner candy store. That is why once again we shall see the peaceful evening shadow steal softly down the street where now only the shadows of the grim people lurks. That is why we will build our homes again that now stand in dead silouette against the flaming sky reminiscent of the day long past. or sit in the cool evening twilight fearing not for the blazing roar of the cannon or bombs half crazed laughter of a hangman power mad. We are rising again and shall continue to do so until the world is rid of those who prey against us. until peace is restored to Gods Earth and all men can resume again the happy normality of Life. Let us not at this precious moment relax our vigulonce or our strength. With victory in sight and peace just around the bend. Let us work harder then ever to bring a smashing defeat to those who would destroy us. Let us rid the world once and for all of those who are the undesirebles.

But there just isn't any mail. What hurts most its almost two months since I got your last letter. We think the fellows from India will bring our mail. They are supposed to be here the 23rd or 26th with all the planes so we sure are sweating the mail out. April 28, 1945 Well at last the mail came. With all our planes here safely. It only took them 16 hours to come from China. I got 38 letters. We pulled a mission on May 6. 16 planes took off; all but one hit primary targets with wonderful results. May 8. A lot of rumors are floating around

But there just what hurts the 2 mo's since we. Thing the India will be suppose be here with all the are sweating the well at last the all our planes only took them from China, I letters, we on May 5th 16 but one hit and wonderfull a lot of roumors

isent any mail is most its almost got your last letter fellows from our mail they are the 23 or 26 the planes so we sure mail out. April 28 mail come with here safely it 16 hrs to come got thirty eight pulled a mission planes took all primeary target results, May 8 are floating around

D.U.S.A.

Hon: Sargeant Dusa: Congratulations! Also regards to your good wife. How is everything coming along? Thanks for your very interesting letter of the 1st. Say congratulations again on the announcement-- I suppose the "Band played On"-- you know thats what we said about Bill V. I wonder how the old Cooky is anyway. Do you ever hear from him?

Guess we are going to get 3 more new Refers. Boy that will created a sensation to see a couple more of those things. Remember when we knocked out 7 in 1 day. Sure showed those Engstrom boys. Boy hurry and help get this war over with so we can get going again. Well was out on the big bond drive. You know I help the home front, sign up recruits, got one for $5000.00 not bad eh?

Well pardon the long delay and hope we will be and in the meantime write.

So long,

Les

MAIL CALL

From Martin Dusa, Jr., somewhere in India, comes this letter:
Dear Les,
 I thought I would drop you a line and thank you for the Pioneer. It was the first I have received here in India and it is dated Jan. 21st. But out here, in almost no man's land, it is all still news of home.
 In my travels thus far, I have seen many interesting things, including wild beasts and snakes. You talk about hunting, boy, it's here, and I mean yellow bellies, too!
 We do eat good, however and have expert medical care.
 Les, I do appreciate the paper very much. Please keep sending it and greet all the folks for me.
 I must close and get ready for another night. Best wishes to you. Your friend, Martin Dusa, rj

GAMBLE STORES INCORPORATED

BUYING OFFICES
ROOMS 808 & 810
200 FIFTH AVENUE
NEW YORK 10, N. Y.

1491 MERCHANDISE MART
CHICAGO 54, ILLINOIS

1100 SOUTH GRAND AVENUE
LOS ANGELES 54, CALIF.

HOME OFFICE
700 WASHINGTON AVE. NORTH
MINNEAPOLIS 1, MINN.

IN REPLY
PLEASE REFER TO

July 18, 1945

Dear Martin:

Thanks a lot for your letter. You are really doing some traveling and are finding out that there is a lot more space to this old world than the average layman could ever imagine. I hope that your points will soon permit your return. You are to be heartily congratulated, with the rest of your outfit, with the presidential citation. I guess you don't get those battle stars for just sitting around.

I understand Les Norgaard is back on the job and feeling pretty well again. He had a bad siege they tell me, but apparently everything turned out right.

Don't know of anything that you haven't heard about as I understand you get the Tiger. Oh, yes, you might be interested in knowing that we placed eight combines on sale at South Dakota during our anniversary this week that sell at about $1700 per copy, and I guess there are a lot of buyers, so every interested person is registered, and then we will draw to see who gets the combines. That is a screwy way to sell, isn't it? I guess such methods won't endure for long after the end of the war as there will be competition again and plenty of merchandise. You have had experience in appliance sales, and I thought you would be interested in that little salesman's prayer item.

Mahlon Rotzien, who was formerly supervisor in Missouri, and who served in the Personnel Department for a time, is now in charge of our outside sales program. You may know Mahlon, as his folks have a cottage at Clitherall, which is in the vicinity of Alexandria and he no doubt stopped at the store on his visits there. He is a grand fellow, and has a lot of spirit. I am sure there will be things happening in the outside sales department. You will enjoy working with him, and I know he is looking forward to your coming back.

Business continues strong, for which we are happy, of course. We'll enjoy business a lot more when it returns to normalcy,

- 2 -

with a lot of the good old fellows like yourself back and on the job.

Just happened to think that now that you have a speaking acquaintance with India, that you may have been able to confirm the authenticity of the Bengal tiger story I told to a bunch of unbelievers in Alexandria—remember? I am sure that if you don't remember it that Les would be glad to give you all the details.

We are reading big things in the papers about the air power that is being turned loose on the Japs. It sounds terrific and it may be even more so than it sounds. We hope that it will soon tell on the Japs to the extent that they throw in the sponge.

Thanks again for the letter and keep writing.

Sincerely,

Kirk

Arnold Kirkness-v

 GAMBLE-SKOGMO INC.

OPERATING

GAMBLE STORES

STORE NUMBER: ALEXANDRIA, MN. 23

CITY: SACRAMENTO, CA

DATE: 12-3-42

Dear Martin & Vi:

Going to sit down and write a few letters tonight-or die in the attempt-boy I am a poor stick to write(undless is it is Blue Sheet letters-haha) Got enough experience on that you know.

Was sure nice to hear from you and that you arrived back safe and sound-werent you kind of lonesome for the oldskate Vi-so far away from home and everything. (Vi--be sure and read the above line right) looks kind of screwy to me now) but you know what I mean, guess I am getting tired.

Would like to see you kids out there in your new home. How is everything, good as ever/

Jack Ley is working for us now-you remember him-andthat with the new girl on the floor helps us out pretty good-still got Bob and Arndt yet. Arndt goes into the local selective service here the 1st.

Hope that you get your Sargents rating, you know they cant keep a good man down--Wish you were back here, would make you a Captain right off the bat-better tell you officer that-

Well there isnt much news to write about-sure has been cold here the last couple days-envy you kids out there now/ Well write when you find time and give us the news. Got the $10.00, thanks a lot.

As ever,

Les

about the war ending in Europe but it is all not confirmed. Yes, today May 9 it has been officially announced the end of the European War. Everyone was very happy. But it doesn't affect us very much as there isn't a darn thing to drink. All the Japs are in the stockade and talk about dirt people. A lot are Koreans – about 5000 here. Everyone here is still on the lookout for the loose ones. Almost each night the guards kill a few. We are getting set up for another raid. There are almost 1000 B29's here and a total of six airfields on Tinian. Each day fighters travel in 24's day and night, and you can see Saipan just a little ways off. I have been here just a few days over a month. Well your reporter must go to bed until more news Goodnight. Well, today, June 10, 1945 About a week ago we were preparing for a mission and I went out to the line with Maj. Thursting one evening. We watched about 80 planes take off when all of a sudden a large red light lit up the sky on the North Field. Yes, it was a B29. It exploded with a full load of incendiaries. Everyone was killed and for an hour the bombs were going off. Then one of our planes whizzed past the tour on a take off

about the war. But its all still yes today 9th affically anounced war. every one But it dosent effect as there isent drink. all the stockades, and dist people a about 5000 here still on the lose ones also. the Gaurds kill getting set for There are almost 6 air fields on

day fighters travel and you can see little ways off Just a couple days your report must go news Goodnight about a week ago for a mission and line with Maj. watched about all of a sudden light up the field yes a B.29 full load of Insen Killed and for a going off. then whized past the

Ending in Europe un confirmed. it has been the end of Europe was very happy et us much a darn thing to Japs are in talk about lot are Koreans every one is look out for the t each night afew. we are anouther raid 1000 B29³ here and tinian each

in 24³ day + night Jipan just a I have been here over a month. Well to bed until more well today June 10, 1945 we were prepairing I went out to the Thursting so we 85 planes when a large red light sky on the North exploded with its tirries every one was hr the Bombs were one of our planes tore on a take off

V-E Day ended war, Third Reich, European conflict

May 8, 1945.

President Truman and Prime Minister Winston Churchill proclaimed it V-E Day — Victory in Europe.

The war in the Pacific would rage on nearly five more months. But to the delirious throngs in Times Square and every big and small town in America, V-E Day meant no more Hitler, Himmler, black shirts, brown shirts or goose-stepping.

World War II had begun 5½ years earlier, on Sept. 1, 1939, when almost 2 million German troops swarmed across the Polish border. Russia attacked from the east. Two days later Britain and France declared war on Germany. But Poland fell in just 30 days.

"Blitzkrieg," German for lightning war, instantly entered the vocabularies of all the world's nations.

World War II — not just a war, but an epoch, really — produced some of the most heroic and most barbarous events in human history. The toll in lives has been estimated as high as 50 million. The Soviet Union alone lost 20 million, the Germans nearly 5 million, the Japanese 2 million. The British and French each had half a million dead, the United States about 300,000.

The passage of 40 years has scarcely

The Associated Press

An American soldier searches a surrendering member of Germany's elite guard, the SS, at the Elba River.

1945

Jan. 12 — Despite stubborn German resistance, the Russians drive into Poland and seize Warsaw and other major cities.

Feb. 7 — An ailing Roosevelt meets Churchill and Stalin at Yalta to plan the defeat of Germany and draft the outlines of peace.

March 7 — Americans cross the Rhine. Shortly afterward, Russians reach Berlin.

February-March — The bloody struggle for Iwo Jima gives the Allies a base within striking distance of the Japanese mainland. Of 30,000 U.S. Marines in the assault, 20,000 are killed or wounded.

March — American forces invade Okinawa, the fiercest struggle of the Pacific conflict. By June, more than 12,000 Americans and 110,000 Japanese are dead. Kamikaze planes inflict heavy damage to the U.S. fleet. Victory is followed by a massive air offensive against Japanese cities and the remnants of the Japanese fleet.

Anne Frank, 15, dies of typhus at the Bergen-Belsen death camp, two months before its liberation.

April 12 — Roosevelt dies of a cerebral hemorrhage at age 63 in Warm Springs, Ga. Vice President Truman succeeds him as president.

April — The German army in Italy surrenders unconditionally. Mussolini is killed trying to escape anti-Fascist partisans.

April 30 — Hitler and his bride, Eva Braun, commit suicide. No bodies are ever found. Nazi propagandist Josef Goebbels likewise kills himself.

May 1 — With Berlin under siege, German radio announces Hitler is dead.

May 7 — German army chiefs go to Eisenhower's headquarters at a red schoolhouse at Reims and sign a surrender.

May 8 — Truman proclaims the end of the war in Europe.

July 17-Aug. 2 — Truman, Churchill and Stalin meet at Potsdam to discuss peace plans. The allies also issue an ultimatum to Japan warning of its "complete ... destruction" unless it unconditionally surrenders. Japan rejects the warning.

Aug. 6 — The first atomic bomb is dropped on Hiroshima; 78,000 are dead, 14,000 missing, 37,000 injured.

Aug. 8 — The Soviet Union, which agreed at Potsdam to join forces with the United States in the Pacific if Japan didn't surrender, declares war on Japan.

Aug. 9 — A second atomic bomb falls on Nagasaki.

Sept. 2 — The Japanese formally surrender on the *USS Missouri* — V-J Day.

with one engine on fire. Of course it was too late to stop so Capt. Makovic, the pilot, got out over the water and everyone bailed out and the Navy patrol boat picked them all up. But the plane exploded in the air over the water. Then almost the last plane to leave got to the end of the runway and something went wrong and he had to drop his bombs and what a fire that was. But nobody got hurt and he made a good landing. Then on the North Field again another explosion so we jumped into the jeep and sped down there. A B29 ran off the runway and exploded. Just two came out alive. That all happened in one night. And about midnight I just got back and saw a plane coming in to land. He couldn't make the trip to Tokyo so he came back. I stepped out of my tent and all I could see was a big explosion with bombs bursting. Boy that night I will never forget. The whole island shook. So in three days we lost Maj. Ellerbie over the target Tokyo, a big loss for us and the tales are endless of the operations. On June 6 we opened our mess hall for the officers. General Ramey and General McDonald from Saipan came to visit my mess

with one Engine on fire of course its too late to stop so Capt Makovic the piolt got out over the water and every one Bailed out and the navey petrol Boat picked them all up But plane exploded in the air over the water, then almost the last plane to leave got to the end of the runaway and something went wrong he had to drop his load of Bombs and what a fire that was But no body got hurt he made a good landing then on the north field again another explosion so we jumped into the Jeep and speed down their and a 29 ran off the runaway and exploded. Just two came out alive that all happend one night and about midnight I just got back and seen a plane coming in to land, he couldent make the trip to toyko is he came back and I stiped out side my tent and all I could see was a Big explosion and Bombs Bursting Boy that night I will never forget the whole Island Shook that was the 21st of May. that night so in About three day we lost Maj Ellerbie over the target toyko. a by lose to us. and tails are endless of the operations. on June 6th we opened our mess all for the officers and Gen Ramey & Gen O'Donell from sipian cone to visit my mess.

219

and paid high compliments. They said it was the best they had ever seen. Col Kalberer has thanked me many times for the fine work. He made me the decorator inside and out. I am glad I got away from the entire responsibilities of running the mess. I am now building a little coffee shop adjoining the officers mess. Gee the place in general is sure looking different each day with good roads, food, and mail service isn't bad. I have two Jap prisoners working for me hauling sand and they do the dirty work like cleaning the garbage rack, etc. So until further happenings Goodnight for June 10, 1945.

and paid high compliments and said its the finest he has seen, and the Col Kaleberer has thanked me many times for the fine work, and so he made me the decorator inside & out I am glad I got away from the entire responsibility of running the mess so now I am building a little coffee shop adjoining the officers mess. The the place is looking different General is sure each day good roads and food and mess service isn't bad I have two Jap prisoners working for me hauling sand and they do the dirty work, clean Garbage rack etc. Until further happenings Good night for June 10, 1945 10:20 PM

JUNE 10, 1945
TINIAN

SGT. MARTIN DUSA, FOURTH FROM LEFT

NEW OFFICERS' MESS – TINIAN
S/SGT. MARTIN DUSA – FOURTH FROM LEFT

---- BATTLE LINES ----
TWO AGUIJAN JAPS VISIT TINIAN UNDER TRUCE

TINIAN —Although living within sight of Tinian's busy B-29 base, several hundred Japanese military, civilians, holding out on the by-passed island of Aguijan, five miles south of here, had had no news of the outside world for nearly a year until negotiations for their surrender began last week.

While the island's commander appeared credulous when Lt. John G. Reifsnider, Naval Intelligence officer, told him of the Emperor's capitulation order, he declined to sign formal surrender documents until he had heard news from Japanese sources. Lt. Reifsnider, landed on Aguijan from an LCM for his talks with the Japanese officer.

As a result, under a flag of truce, two Japanese non-coms boarded a Coast Guard cutter which brought them to Tinian where, after a six-hour vigil, they heard a Radio Tokyo broadcast of the Emperor's instructions to his troops.

These preparations for the surrender negotiations were under the direction of Col. Robert C. Pixton, Iscom G-3.

* * *

From S/SGT. MARTIN DUSA in the Marianas
Formerly at Alexandria, Minn.

I still am in the B29 outfit and like my work very much. We just received the Presidential Citation, and four battle stars, so I am waiting for my turn to come to the states sometime this fall. When the day comes that I land in San Francisco, that will complete a trip around the world for me. At the present time I am on Tinian in the Marianas. The climate is very good, and our rations are so much better than in India. We manage to get a few cans of beer a week.

JULY GAMBLES TIGER

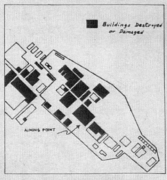

THANKS MEN! YOUR WORK PAID OFF

BEFORE — DURING

HIRO NAVAL AIRCRAFT FACTORY
KURE, WESTERN HONSHU
58th BOMB WING MISSION NO. 1 5-MAY-1945

MAY 24-26, 1945 MISSIONS DESTROY OVER 18.6 SQ MI. OF TOKYO
58 BOMBING WING PLANES

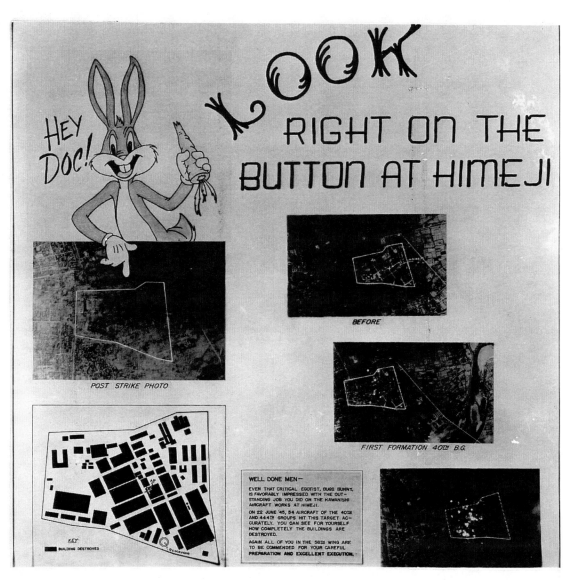

JUNE 22, 1945
PLANES OF THE 58 BOMB WING
KAWANISHI AIRCRAFT WORKS

Armorers in the process of loading and arming M69 500-lb incendiary clusters in the bomb bay of a B-29. It was clusters such as these which made the fire blitz raids against Japan so devastating. (AAF POA)

In spite of severe tail damage, aircraft 3846 of the 504th Bomb Group returned to Tinian after 16 July 1945 mission.

HEADQUARTERS
TWENTIETH AIR FORCE
WASHINGTON 25, D. C.

GENERAL ORDERS)
)   15 June 1945
NO.   8   )   A W A R D S

I - - DISTINGUISHED UNIT CITATION. - - As authorized by Executive Order 9396 superseding Executive Order 9075, and under the provisions of Section IV, Circular No. 333, War Department 1943, the following units of the XX Bomber Command are cited for outstanding performance of duty in action against the enemy:

* *

462ND BOMBARDMENT GROUP (VH), XX BOMBER COMMAND, is cited for outstanding performance of duty in armed conflict with the enemy on 20 August 1944. The group dispatched ****B-29 type aircraft to its forward bases to be disposed in two groups on D-Day as part of the XX Bomber Command mission. One-half of the group carried out a special night attack following the all out XX Bomber Command daylight precision attack. Fighter opposition was successfully overcome on the way to the target. Despite a steady hail of intense and accurate flak concentrations which accounted for damage to two aircraft which caused them to crash on the return run to their forward bases, and despite continuous enemy fighter attacks employing suicide ramming tactics, the 462nd Group succeeded in destroying the Imperial Iron and Steel Works at Yawata on the Jap mainland. In the accomplishment of its primary mission, six enemy aircraft were damaged or destroyed. The success of its part of the mission by the 462nd Bombardment Group was especially outstanding in that the method of attack used called for the utmost in daring and skill. The first daylight raid over the Japanese home islands since the historic raid of Tokyo in April 1942 proved the real effectiveness of daylight precision bombing by B-29's. The hazards of mechanical failure, fighter opposition, flak and barrage balloons on the mission of over 3,000 miles were all overcome by the valor and high professional ability of all members of the 462nd Bombardment Group and by their courage, cooperative spirit and tireless energy, the individuals of this Group have reflected great credit on themselves and the Army Air Forces.

* *

By command of General ARNOLD:

PRESIDENTIAL CITATION
LAURIS NORSTAD,
Brigadier General, U. S. Army
Chief of Staff

OFFICIAL:

s/ H. H. Hewitt
t/ H. H. HEWITT
Lieutenant Colonel, A.G.D.,
Adjutant General.

A CERTIFIED TRUE EXTRACT COPY

Arch C Fleming
ARCH C. FLEMING,
Captain, Air Corps.

June 13, 1945 Today our 462 Bomb Group or should I say the 58th Wing which consists of 440th, 444th, 468th, 462nd, Bomb Groups make up the 58th Wing. Each Group has 48 planes and each Sqd has 15 planes to take care of. In our Group 768, 769, 770, and HQ. The whole Wing received the Presidential Citation. Today June 16 General Hap Arnold visited the base on Tinian. July 12 we had an earthquake. It shook the whole island and all the dishes in the mess hall fell. July 13 The planes went on a mission. One of our planes was going down the runway at full speed on take off and couldn't lift. It fell off the end of the runway and all 11 got out and one minute later the plane blew into a million pieces. One fellow had a broken foot. Today we had General Ramey for coffee at the shop and he said very nice. Today I got official authorization on my 4th Battle Star and 86 points so am waiting for a replacement. July 17 today we had a scare near the hospital. Our guards killed six armed Japs and 11 prisoners so we still have them on the island. July 18 today we had our Group picture taken. It will be entered in our Yearbook. Today I took over as Mess SGT and made out my first menu. Tonight I had a special supper made for the Col. and his staff. They were talking over post war ideas for the HELLBIRDS.

At 5:30 just a

June 13, 1945 today should I say the consist of 440th 444th make up the 58 wing and each sq has 15 thats in our gp the whole wing citation. today visited the base we had a Earth quake Island. and all the mess hall, July a mission on going down the run on take off, and it fell of the end of all 1 got out and the plane blew to one fellow had a we had Gen Ram shop and said very official authorization and 86 points, so I July 17, today we Hospital they killed prisoners. so we on the Island. had our group picture be entered in our today, I took over as out my first menu a special supper made they are talking over for the "Hell Birds"

our 462 Bomb gp or 58th wing which 468 & 462 Bomb gp each gp has 48 planes planes to take care off 768, 769, + 770, + Hq. recieved the presedantual June 16. Gen H H arnold on tinian. July 12 it shook the whole dishes fell in the 13, plane went on of our planes was away at full speed couldn't lift to the runaway and one minute later a million pieces broken foot. today my for coffee at the nice. today I got an my 4th Battle Star waiting for a replacement had a day near the 6 armed japs & we still have them July 18, today we taken. it will year Book. and mess sgt and make and tonight I had for the Col. & his staff post war Ideas, and at 5:30 just a

WHEN A GROUP OF AMERICANS ARE BROUGHT TOGETHER INTO A MILITARY ORGANIZATION UNDER THE CONDITIONS GOVERNING THAT MOBILIZATION - THE DEFENSE OF THEIR COUNTRY, THEIR HOMES AND THEIR WAY OF LIFE AGAINST AN INSIDIOUS ENEMY THERE DEVELOPS NOT ONLY A TIGHTLY KNIT ORGANIZATION OF FIGHTING MEN BUT A FRATERNITY OF INDIVIDUALS. MEN LIVING TOGETHER, WORKING, GRIPING AND FIGHTING TOGETHER BECOME A UNIT WITH A CHARACTER . . . AN ENTITY!

...SUCH ARE THE HELLBIRDS.

air and sea voyages of hellbirds in world war II

TINIAN EXPERIMENT

The island of Tinian is gradually being cleared of Japs by the novel method of getting them to surrender instead of shooting them one by one.

By Cpl. JUSTIN GRAY
YANK Staff Correspondent

Beginning

THE MARIANAS—The daily news sheet on the tiny island of Tinian in the Marianas carried the item just to fill space. No one took much notice of it:

"Fourteen Japanese soldiers were captured today on Tinian by our troops."

The news sheet didn't even bother to tell the full story. But both the editor and the GI readers knew the story well by now. The surrender of 14 Japanese soldiers was no longer news on Tinian. The Japs had been surrendering in equal numbers for the past six weeks.

The story began about two months ago when three Seabees decided to take a walk through a "safe" area on the western end of the island to look for souvenirs. No Japs had been reported in this vicinity for months. B-29s had been taking off regularly for their attacks on Tokyo from runways just a few hundred yards away. The men saw no reason to carry arms. While still in sight of their bivouac area two of the sailors were killed and the third was wounded by a group of well-armed Japanese who ambushed them.

Immediate routine steps were taken to round up these Japanese. Although the island had long since been officially "secured," the presence of any group of armed Japs was a threat to the security of the B-29s and to our other installations in the area. The 24th Infantry Regiment moved out for another sweep across the island.

But back at headquarters Maj. Charles F. Erb Jr., of Los Angeles, chief of G-2, who had ordered this infantry sweep, began to formulate a new and possibly revolutionary technique aimed at neutralizing rapidly and efficiently the remaining Japanese opposition on Tinian.

Maj. Erb, quarterback on the great undefeated University of California football team way back in 1920 and '21, was no armchair strategist. He had flown on as many missions as the average pilot and he had gone out on numerous patrols with the 24th Infantry during the original securing of the island. The major understood the problems of the foot soldier on a job like this sweep. He knew the Japs could hide in spots impossible for an infantryman to find. He felt almost certain this latest attempt would produce no conclusive gains. The very fact that we had been patrolling the island for eight months and that Japs still remained proved this point.

In addition, the infantrymen of the 24th, who were doing this cleaning up on Tinian, had been overseas 37 months. This was no time to risk lives foolishly. Something new had to be tried.

"I was interested at this time in two things," explained Maj. Erb. "First, it was necessary to neutralize the Japanese opposition on the island in the quickest possible time so that our base might operate with peak efficiency. It seemed obvious to me that the infantry would have to work months and maybe years in order to search and clean out all the possible caves. And second, I wanted to accomplish this operation with a minimum amount of loss of life on our part."

Since the traditional method of blasting the Japs out of their caves was not too successful the only other method available was to convince the Japs they should surrender voluntarily. This on the surface looked almost impossible. Up to this date our psychological warfare program hadn't produced much results. Either the Japs were fanatical or they feared us—maybe it was a combination of both—but our leaflets and broadcasts seemed of little value.

Maj. Erb, nevertheless, decided to try an experiment in psychological warfare.

HE had a new twist to the idea. Previously Americans with a knowledge of Japanese had been making our broadcasts and other appeals to the Japanese soldiers. Their accent left something to be desired and, as might be expected, the Japs rarely trusted their words. The major wanted to go right to the resisting Japanese and appeal to them directly. His plan was to use Japanese PWs themselves to make this contact.

One problem was, of course, to find a PW willing and able to return to the hills in order to convince his friends they should surrender. The major had a second problem in convincing his superiors that a PW should be released for such work. Surprisingly enough, it was easier for him to convince the Jap PW than it was to sell the idea to the Americans.

The U. S. soldier has been conditioned never to trust a Jap. "A good Jap is a dead Jap" is the phrase most easily said and understood. But Major Erb finally got permission to try his experiment and set about looking for "his Jap."

Fortunately he didn't have to wait long. The infantry, in their sweep across the island, trapped a number of Japs and after throwing a satchel charge into their hiding spot managed to disarm a few before they could get over their stunned condition. Out of this group Maj. Erb chose one who seemed tough and arrogant and a leader. The major knew for his experiment to be a success he would have to use a Jap who would command respect and possibly a bit of fear from his fellow countrymen. CONT.

The job of convincing the Jap PW—now called Tuffy by everyone on Tinian—was much easier than the major had dared to hope. No political indoctrination was necessary. The mere fact we did not kill him but instead fed and clothed him well was sufficient to change Tuffy from an arrogant bitter enemy to a cooperative and happy prisoner. In fact Tuffy had been our prisoner only one day before he volunteered to go out to bring back some of his friends.

This was a crucial time for Maj. Erb's experiment. Almost everyone was sceptical and fearful of the results. The very thought of letting a PW roam around on his own upset those who thought strictly in terms of the ARs. Actually sending Tuffy out alone did have dangerous implications which could not be ignored. Tuffy had seen our installations at first hand and this information could have been of great value to the enemy. There was the possibility Tuffy might return not as a friend but as the leader of a raiding party.

On the other hand, if Tuffy was actually going to try to bring in some of his friends this was also a crucial moment for him. Tuffy had been instructed exactly what to tell his friends. He was to tell them of his own treatment and the fact that we would not kill others if they decided to come back with him. These were the same facts we had presented to the resisting Japanese in our earlier attempts in psychological warfare. There was no assurance Tuffy's friends would take kindly to these old arguments. They might well consider Tuffy a traitor to the Emperor and kill him instead.

Tuffy must have been a good salesman for he returned from his first "patrol" with eight new PWs. He seemed to have had a hard time convincing them, for he was white and shaken as he crossed the clearing to the spot where Maj. Erb and the official observers waited. The new PWs were also shaking for even though they had been swayed by Tuffy's arguments they still were not thoroughly sold on the truth of his story.

The eight new arrivals were given the same treatment Tuffy had the day before. Soon some Japs from this group volunteered to help Tuffy in future "patrols." And so the program expanded.

At the end of the first six weeks of Maj. Erb's program exactly 313 Japanese soldiers had voluntarily given up to Tuffy and his fellow PWs. In all this time not a single shot was fired either by us or the Japs. Not one Jap who went into the hills failed to return to the stockade at the end of his "patrol." Not one PW was ever hurt by other Japs for being a "traitor to the Emperor."

EACH day at 1030 a "patrol" of PWs left the stockade on Tinian and moved out into the hills to bring in more of the remaining Japanese. The other day I went out on one of these patrols and watched Tuffy return with 16 additional Jap soldiers. These men weren't even frightened. They had heard through the grapevine of our good treatment of their fellow soldiers. On questioning they admitted having considered coming out of the hills and surrendering themselves but they thought it best to wait until they could contact Tuffy and come out with him.

"This is a far cry from the time Tuffy first went out for us," enthusiastically explained T-4 Charles T. Nicolosi of Gloucester, Mass., who has been working very closely with Maj. Erb on this program. "The first Japs to surrender were frightened half to death. They honestly believed we were barbaric people and would torture them. Now that we have shown this Japanese propaganda line to be a lie they are as willing to surrender as anyone else. We're really getting results now."

Japanese propagandists, of course, have stimulated artificially a good portion of this "fear the American" attitude among their civilians and military, but we ourselves have given the Japanese added fuel for their "propaganda line."

IN the early days of the war we fought at close quarters with the Japs in the jungles of the South Pacific and on the small coral atolls of the Central Pacific. Under such conditions it was impossible either for the Japs to surrender or for us to capture many even if we so desired. Because we didn't understand the Jap soldier and his oriental outlook on life we looked down upon him as being something inferior. We found it easy to kill at random. Units that took no prisoners won the reputation of being tough. It wasn't long before it became the accepted thing not to take Japanese PWs.

Now that our victories have mounted to such a crescendo that the Japs might consider surrendering in large numbers we find that our past policy of not taking prisoners stands in their way.

The work being accomplished on the island of Tinian is of course only a small item in terms of the large numbers of Japanese we are facing on the battlefields. But it serves as some indication of what may be accomplished on the battlefield if we begin an all-out program of psychological warfare.

"From our interrogation of PWs," said Maj. Erb, "everything indicates the Japanese troops fight fanatically and refuse to surrender not so much because of Emperor worship but rather because they fear death and torture in our hands. Show the Jap we are not going to kill him and he will surrender. That puts it squarely up to us."

As usual the hardest and dirtiest portion of the job falls upon the shoulders of the infantrymen. Radio broadcasts can be made and leaflets dropped but in the last analysis it is still up to the foot soldier to do the actual capturing of the Jap. This isn't going to be easy at the beginning. There is doubt the Jap soldier—and the same probably holds true for the civilian—still intends to resist being captured even if he has to kill himself. Most Japs still believe they will be tortured or killed if they fall into our hands. But with each additional Japanese soldier neutralized as a PW the task of achieving victory will be that much easier. Mass surrender of the Japanese military is a prerequisite for an early peace. Mass surrender is possible only if the American infantryman gives the Jap soldier the opportunity to surrender.

Tue & Wed — Aug 29-30

Supper	Breakfast	Dinner
Vegtable Soup	Tomato Juice	Cold Corn Beef
Crotoons	Fried Eggs	Lynnoise potatoes
Fried Steak	Fried Bacon	Baild Corn on cob
French fried potatoes	Oat Meal	Buttered Beans
Brown Gravy	Coffee	Sliced Onions
Creamed Corn		Fruit Cocktail
Buttered Carrots		Ice cocoa
Pickles		
Cuc. Salad		
Ice Cream		
Chocolate Cake		
Punch		
Cherry wine		
Coffee		

1st Cook Jackson

All Cook & KP's & Waiters will help tonight on General table.

Mess Sgt. D usa.

half mile from the mess hall a B29 crashed; killed all 11 men on board outright. It just flew very low over the mess hall with two engines on fire. That's all for today. July 20 one of our planes crashed at the end of the runway on take off. Everyone got out and it blew into a million pieces; the co-pilot got killed. July 21 Today I received a very nice letter of commendation from Col Kalberer Today August 7 the first Atomic Bomb hit the target. They took off from North Field Bombing 313 Wing. And today August 9 Russia is at war with Japan. The second Atomic Bomb hit Nagasaki. Yesterday at mission time at 2 in the morning it was raining. The first two planes cracked up; one on each runway, so they cancelled the mission. On August 7 I had a big feed for General Spann and staff; it went over big. That's all for today. August 10 Gee rumors have it that Japan is about to stop. We, from here, dropped the Atomic Bomb. August 14 No word yet from Japan. Today I got a hell of a nasty letter from my wife about her working at a night club. Oh well more for next time. August 19 Today things much the same. I wrote Aunt Faye about Vi's working at a night club. Well, things are changing. We are painting the underside of the wings on our planes

half mile from the killed all 11 men sad very low over the mess Engines on fire

July 20. one of our the End of the every one got out a million pieces killed. July 21 today nice letter of conc today aug 7 the hit the target tape of 313 wing. and Russia is at war the second atomic and yesterday at mission it was raining

planes craped up so they Couscelled took off today. and a big feed for it went over big aug 16. see rumors is about to stop droped atomic bomb no work yet from I got a hell of a my wife about night club club next time. aug 19. much the same I wrote I/2 working at a night are slowly changing under side of our

mess Hall a B29 crashed write. it just flew half with two that's all for today. planes crashed at runaway on take off and it Blew in the Co-pilot got I received a very comedation from Col. Hal. first atomic Bomb off from north field today aug 9th with Japan and Bomb hit Nagasaki time at 2 in morning and the first two

one on Each runaway the mission and on the 7th I had Gen Spats & staff thats all for today. have it that Japan and we from here and today aug 17. and Japan. and today nasty letter from her working at a so swell more for today sunday things aunty faye a letter about Club. Well things are painting the wing on our planes.

HEADQUARTERS 462ND BOMBARDMENT GROUP
APO 247, c/o Postmaster
San Francisco, California

21 July 1945

201-Dusa, Martin (Enl)

SUBJECT: Commendation

TO: S/Sgt Martin Dusa, 17 049 855
Headquarters, 462nd Bombardment Group
APO 247, c/o Postmaster
San Francisco, California

    All too often the services rendered by personnel working in Army messes are overlooked, no matter how excellent the performance. In your case, however, the results achieved have been so outstanding at all times that they cannot escape notice.

    During the nearly unbearable heat of last summer in India, when you took over the officer's mess, you managed somehow to overcome the obstacles created by the long supply lines and turn out tasty meals, making this mess one of the finest in the entire XX Bomber Command. Later when the Group moved to Tinian new obstacles arose in establishing a consolidated Group Mess, which because of its size made severe demands on your time and initiative. Throughout the early days on this island, facilities were few and your enthusiastic application to duty as mess sergeant helped to keep the morale of this command high.

    In addition to the natural difficulties overcome, it was necessary to feed the officers as well as the enlisted men in this mess inasmuch as a separate mess had not then been established, thus causing additional effort on the part of mess personnel. You may take pride in the fact that in the face of all these difficulties, Major General Jones made a personal inspection tour of the 462nd mess and adjudged it the finest in the 58th Bombardment Wing.

    Since the establishment of the officers mess and your transfer thereto, you have continued to maintain the same enthusiastic and diligent attention to duty which has always been characteristic of your work, and consequently the same high standards have resulted in the new mess hall.

    I have no doubt your efficiency after the war in civil life will equal that you have shown during this period of your country's peril and sincerely hope your post-war life is a good one.

    For the foregoing and for your exemplary devotion to duty at all times, you are due the highest commendation. I also wish to add the thanks of the Group and my personal regards.

Sincerely,

ALFRED F. KALBERER
Colonel, Air Corps
Commanding

HEADQUARTERS 462ND BOMBARDMENT GROUP
APO 247, c/o Postmaster
San Francisco, California

21 July 1945

201-Dusa, Martin (Enl)

SUBJECT: Commendation

TO : S/Sgt Martin Dusa, 17 049 855
Headquarters, 462nd Bombardment Group
APO 247, c/o Postmaster
San Francisco, California

    All too often the services rendered by personnel working in Army messes are overlooked, no matter how excellent the performance. In your case, however, the results achieved have been so outstanding at all times that they cannot escape notice.

    During the nearly unbearable heat of last summer in India, when you took over the officer's mess, you managed somehow to overcome the obstacles created by the long supply lines and turn out tasty meals, making this mess one of the finest in the entire XX Bomber Command. Later when the Group moved to Tinian new obstacles arose in establishing a consolidated Group Mess, which because of its size made severe demands on your time and initiative. Throughout the early days on this island, facilities were few and your enthusiastic application to duty as mess sergeant helped to keep the morale of this command high.

    In addition to the natural difficulties overcome, it was necessary to feed the officers as well as the enlisted men in this mess inasmuch as a separate mess had not then been established, thus causing additional effort on the part of mess personnel. You may take pride in the fact that in the face of all these difficulties, Major General Jones made a personal inspection tour of the 462nd mess and adjudged it the finest in the 58th Bombardment Wing.

    Since the establishment of the officers mess and your transfer thereto, you have continued to maintain the same enthusiastic and diligent attention to duty which has always been characteristic of your work, and consequently the same high standards have resulted in the new mess hall.

    I have no doubt your efficiency after the war in civil life will equal that you have shown during this period of your country's peril and sincerely hope your post-war life is a good one.

    For the foregoing and for your exemplary devotion to duty at all times, you are due the highest commendation. I also wish to add the thanks of the Group and my personal regards.

    Sincerely,

ALFRED F. KALBERER
Colonel, Air Corps
Commanding

The End

TEST OF THE FIRST ATOMIC BOMB sent this cloud of flame into substratosphere. A month later the bomb ended the war.

"MONSTROUS.....SPECTACULAR"

At 9:30 on a beautiful morning, early in August, 1945, history came to the Japanese city of Hiroshima, and death, and a thing so fantastic that men will grope for adjectives to describe it to the end of time.

The flash came first, a great white glare so intense that men 15 miles away could not look upon it with their naked eyes and retain their sight. In a lonely photo recon plane, 175 miles away across Honshu, the crew saw the flash and for a moment thought it was a kind of sunrise. It was more than a sunrise. The glare expanded and then died away in the space of a couple of seconds. For a few thousandths of a second at its peak, the flash had the intensity of 1,000 suns, according to the matter-of-fact measurements of physicists.

The heat of that flash, for its duration, was like nothing known on earth since the planet first cooled, a thing to be measured only in stellar temperatures, thousands of degrees centigrade. It was so hot that life withered in the range of its searing breath. The Japanese said afterwards that live humans all at once were charred and shapeless lumps. Dogs and cats and mice and birds perished, and the green things in the parks of Hiroshima, the vegetables in the gardens, the very bacteria in the air about the city, were destroyed.

Then a great bubble of flame, miles across, formed above the city and catapulted itself into the stratosphere at terrific speed. It seemed to cool as it arose, to pale pink, then the angry red of forced flame, then a dull orange glow and finally to a pure white mushroom. Within three minutes after the explosion, it had shot past the Superforts and now towered high over them, its fleecy top above 40,000 feet.

Simultaneously, enormous shock waves radiated out from the explosion like ripples spreading in a still pool, finishing whatever remained in the center of Hiroshima. With a roar probably unequalled in 70 years—since the explosion of the island of Krakatoa in 1883—the air around the explosion was compressed into a force that hit like a vast sledgehammer as it rushed away from the center in waves of concussion that crumbled walls to powder, crushed wood to pulp, smashed into an unrecognizable mess the thousands of homely articles which the people of Hiroshima used in the business of living—furniture, dishes, drapery, whether elaborate or humble. And when the air rushed back into the vacuum created by the blast, it finished the job. There was little debris in the usual sense of jumbled houses and rubble and smashed beams. This debris was not that sizeable. It was more like dust.

Miles away, men of the B-29s circled the city, watching the thing they had wrought. One of the bombers, the Enola-Gay, was named after the nice, gray-haired mother of its commander, Col Paul W. Tibbets Jr, of Miami. Another was The Great Artiste, so-named by its crew in a burst of jeering affection for their bombardier, Capt. Kermit K. Beahan of Houston, a big, good-natured Texan who had taken a constant ribbing for his alleged prowess with the women, and who was known among experts as one of the greatest bombardiers in the AAF. A third Superfort was crowded with photographers and technical observers.

As the three aircraft had first swung across southern Honshu to approach Hiroshima, their crews had gone through a careful ritual. They donned heavy welders' goggles and those whose duties kept them stationary got into flak suits—the men who had to move around didn't bother. In the Enola-Gay, Col Tibbets held her straight while the bombardier, Maj Thomas W. Ferebee, fiddled with the dials. Elsewhere in the aircraft, a Navy captain, William S. Parsons, made certain vital adjustments on the missile she carried. These three men were the only ones aboard the Enola-Gay who knew what they carried and what it would do. Briefed to expect something sensational, but not aware of what it would be, the rest of the crew busied themselves with their own work. Ferebee fixed her up on the Jap army headquarters, flipped the release when the time came, and then called: "Bomb away." Tibbets pushed the big bomber into a sharp diving turn to pick up speed and put distance between the Enola-Gay and Hiroshima. The crews of all three planes turned away from the windows, faced the interior of

(Continued on next page)

BRIEF ★ 3

ATOMIC BOMB

[The] States War Department was brought [in ... about] 1942 when it appeared that an atomic [bomb could be] developed in time to be of use in World [War II. In] 1943, the U.S. Army Engineers took [charge] of all activities related to the development [of atomic] energy and atomic bombs. The name [was] changed to the Manhattan Engineer [District and] General Leslie R. Groves was appointed [to direct] the project.

[Plants] were built to speed up production of [uranium and] plutonium. Plutonium, element 94, [was produce]d in a nuclear reactor by the bombard[ment of U-238] with neutrons. Special reactors for this [were] built at Hanford, Wash. U-235 was [separated from] U-238 in great plants constructed at [Oak Ridge]. Finally, limited amounts of material [were produced] and purified, ready for use in a bomb. [The ques]tion was whether the bomb would be [effective. To an]swer this, a great scientific laboratory [was built] at Los Alamos, N.M., near Santa Fe. [It] was directed by the young American [Dr. Rob]ert Oppenheimer.

[The bomb] was carefully assembled on a desert [near Alamogord]o, N.M. On July 16, 1945, scientists [and observer]s witnessed from a safe distance the [atomic] explosion. The light from the bomb, [the h]eat and wind rushed out in all direc[tions. Scien]tists later learned that the high steel [tower that] the bomb was placed had disappeared [into] vapor.

[Weeks] later, on August 6, 1945, a United

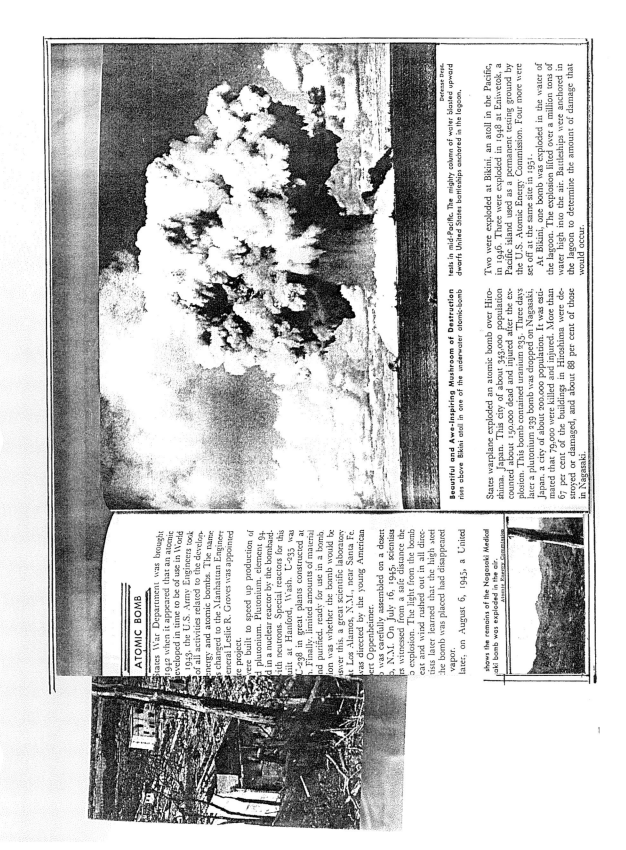

[The picture] shows the remains of the Nagasaki Medical [College after the atom]ic bomb was exploded in the air.
Atomic Energy Commission

Beautiful and Awe-Inspiring Mushroom of Destruction rises above Bikini atoll in one of the underwater atomic-bomb tests in mid-Pacific. The mighty column of water blasted upward dwarfs United States battleships anchored in the lagoon.
Defense Dept.

States warplane exploded an atomic bomb over Hiroshima, Japan. This city of about 343,000 population counted about 150,000 dead and injured after the explosion. This bomb contained uranium 235. Three days later a plutonium 239 bomb was dropped on Nagasaki, Japan, a city of about 200,000 population. It was estimated that 79,000 were killed and injured. More than 67 per cent of the buildings in Hiroshima were destroyed or damaged, and about 88 per cent of those in Nagasaki.

Two were exploded at Bikini, an atoll in the Pacific, in 1946. Three were exploded in 1948 at Eniwetok, a Pacific island used as a permanent testing ground by the U.S. Atomic Energy Commission. Four more were set off at the same site in 1951.

At Bikini, one bomb was exploded in the water of the lagoon. The explosion lifted over a million tons of water high into the air. Battleships were anchored in the lagoon to determine the amount of damage that would occur.

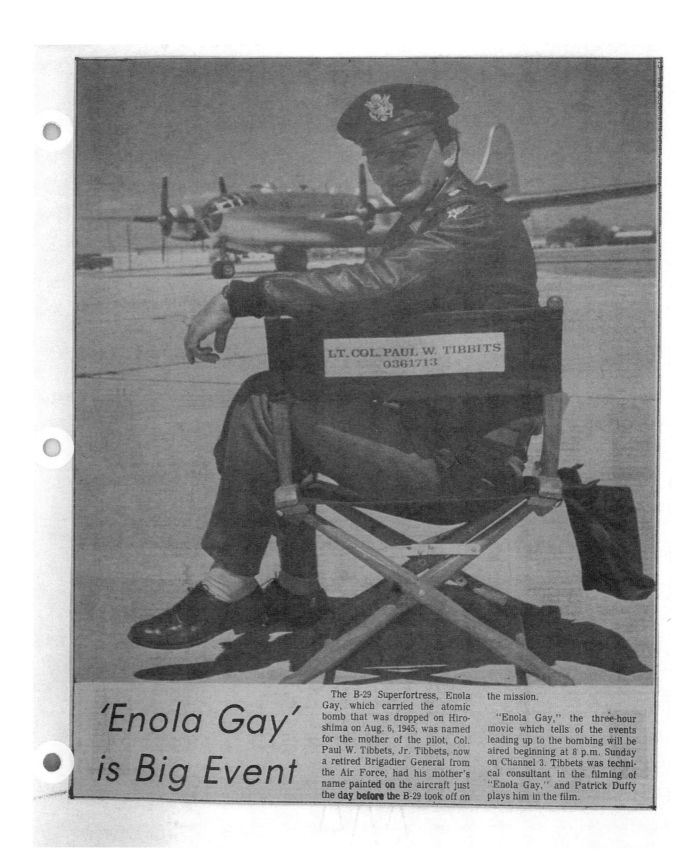

'Enola Gay' is Big Event

The B-29 Superfortress, Enola Gay, which carried the atomic bomb that was dropped on Hiroshima on Aug. 6, 1945, was named for the mother of the pilot, Col. Paul W. Tibbets, Jr. Tibbets, now a retired Brigadier General from the Air Force, had his mother's name painted on the aircraft just the day before the B-29 took off on the mission.

"Enola Gay," the three-hour movie which tells of the events leading up to the bombing will be aired beginning at 8 p.m. Sunday on Channel 3. Tibbets was technical consultant in the filming of "Enola Gay," and Patrick Duffy plays him in the film.

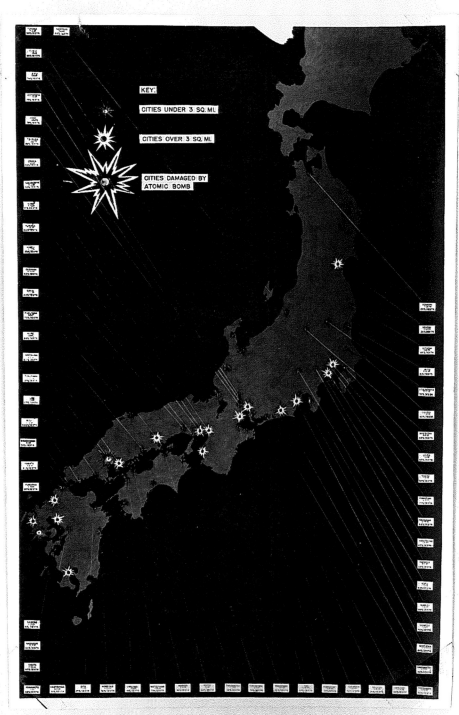

MAP SHOWS SIXTY-ONE TARGETS BOMBED IN JAPAN

The War Started... Then It Ended!

THE ATTACK on Pearl Harbor on Dec. 7, 1941, plunged the United States into war. Japanese aircraft sank 18 ships and killed or wounded 3,681 persons. President Franklin D. Roosevelt signed the declaration of war.

SURRENDER marking the end of World War II came aboard the U.S.S. Missouri in Tokyo Bay, on Sept. 2, 1945. Gen. of the Army Douglas MacArthur, far left, signed for the Allies. Gen. Yoshijiro Umeza signed for the Japanese army.

with the letters P W and SUPPLIES on the other. We plan to ferry prisoners from Manchuria and Japan. No sign of going home yet. That's all for today. August 25 today I had to feed the Charles Ruggles show and troop. I also started to write to Vi again. We also got a rumor that we are going home soon. August 28. Claude Owens left for home. Yes, this is it. August 29. At 10:15 PM the orders just came through for me to pack that I am leaving Aug 30 for home USA. Well we were ready to go so the cancelled it for 48 hours. Today is Sept 2nd, official VE day last night.

with the letters and supplys on the on ferrying prisoners Japan. and no sign that all for today, pinallia for peace. I had to feed the and troop. and I also again. and we also are going home soon. left for Home. yes aug 29 at 10:15 PM. through for me — am leaving aug. Well we were canceled it for. Sept 2nd official

PW on one side outher. and we plan from manchuria & of going home yet. & the Jap party reached signtures. aug 25, today Chas Ruggles show started to write to Vi got a romer that we aug 28, Cloude owens this is it the orders just come to pack that I 30th for Home. 45A. ready to go so they 48 hrs. today is VE day last night

As a direct result of the strikes of the B-29s and the two A-bomb missions, the Japanese government accepted unconditional surrender terms from the Allies on 14 August, and the next day, 15 August 1945, V-J Day. World War II came to an end. Immediately the Twentieth's B-29s turned to peaceful pursuits and began flying POW missions to Japan. Through 20 September there were over twenty such missions on which supplies were dropped to specified POW camps to alleviate suffering until Allied forces could reach the imprisoned men.

Planes of the 9th Bomb Group on POW mission right after the end of the war. "PW SUPPLIES" is printed under wing.

TWENTIETH AIR FORCE MARKINGS

Superforts of the 58th Bomb Wing flew to the CBI and entered combat without having unit markings applied to them. It was not until the first ten days of August 1944 that unit markings were devised and began to be painted on the aircraft. Each group employed its own distinctive pattern. The 40th BG painted the vertical tail tip of its aircraft and four stripes under it in a different color for each of its four squadrons, and placed an aircraft letter on either side of the lower vertical fin. The 444th BG placed a diamond on either side of the upper vertical fin of its B-29s with an aircraft number within it, each squadron having a run of twenty to twenty-five numbers, the run identifying the squadron, the number the aircraft within the squadron. The diamond was black with a white number on NMF aircraft, white with a black number on OD aircraft. The 462nd BG painted the rudders of its planes in a different color for each of its squadrons, and placed a letter high on the vertical fin to identify the aircraft within the squadron. The 468th BG painted two diagonal stripes, usually outlined in black, on the rudders of its B-29s, using a different color for each squadron, and placed a three-digit aircraft number (the last three digits of the serial) above the serial presentation on either side of the vertical fin.

From 10 October 1944, when the groups were reduced from four to three squadrons, the marking system already initiated was continued by the 40th and 468th Groups. The 444th, however, added a vertical band to its planes, painted about the fuselage aft of the wing in a squadron color. The 462nd painted the rudders of all its B-29s red, as a Group marking, retained the aircraft letter on either side of the upper vertical fin and added a squadron identifying number (1, 2 or 3) to either side of the lower vertical fin.

with the high visibility tail markings of other XXI Bomber Command units, a large outlined triangle, identifying the Wing, was painted on either side of the vertical tail of the aircraft in black with a single black letter within it to identify the group, the group letters being S, N, U and I. Individual aircraft were now identified by a black aircraft number painted on either side of the rear fuselage, a run of twenty numbers by the 444th Group, and red group colored rudders were retained by the 462nd Group.

Before the 73rd Bomb Wing departed Kansas to go to Saipan and enter action, a unified unit marking system was devised for its aircraft. This system called for each group to be identified by a group letter placed high on the vertical fin of its aircraft, the wing to be identified by an outlined square placed half-way up the vertical fin but above the serial presentation, and the aircraft within the squadron to be identified by an aircraft number at the bottom of the vertical fin, the run within which the number fell (1-19, 21-39, 41-59) in turn identifying the squadron. From available evidence it appears that at first the four groups were given the group letters A through D, and the new markings were applied to their training aircraft. By the time the overseas aircraft arrived, the group letters A, T, V and Z had been given to the four groups, and employing them, the unit markings were painted in black on either side of the vertical fins of the new planes in a uniform manner throughout the Wing. In the process the serial presentation was deleted, but the last four digits of the serial number were repainted on either side of the rudder in black.

The group letter, square, aircraft number markings remained standard until April 1945 when, to make the tail markings more easily visible, they were superseded by a single large block letter, in black on either side of the vertical tail, each group using the same group letter as before. At the same time the aircraft number was painted in black on either side of the fuselage aft of the national insignia and was usually repeated on either side of the nose. Additionally, aircraft of flight leaders had a black band painted on their dorsal fins or two black

of the barb. In the case of veteran aircraft, the name was usually the one they had previously carried.

When the 313th Bomb Wing arrived on Tinian, its B-29s carried no unit markings. Soon, however, the Wing adopted a markings system like the one first employed by the 73rd, but with an outlined triangle rather than a square as a wing symbol and not over-painting the serial presentation. Group

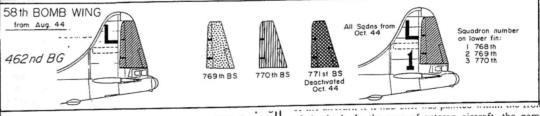

Newly arrived on Tinian, 11 April 1945, 42-24898 of the 462nd Bomb Group, 58th Bomb Wing, is parked by control tower. (USAF)

A B-29 of the 462nd Bomb Group in the markings used by the unit after it joined XXI Bomber Command. On the nose is the group insignia with the inscription, "Hellbirds - With Malice Toward Some".

Hardstands on West Field, Tinian with Superforts of the 462nd Group at left and the 40th Group at right. (AAF)

Sat night we sent out our planes for a VICTORY flight over Tokyo. General Ramey and Col Kal had eaten before they left. I told Col Kal that I was taken off the loading list; that now I had to go by boat. So Col Kal asked the General to have me put back on the list to fly home tomorrow the 3rd of Sept. Now its Sunday noon and waiting for our 40 planes to return about 4:30 this PM. Gee, I can't sleep or eat I am so excited. Well here it is Tues the 4th and still packed and waiting. We were to go to ATC but it was cancelled. This morning I went to the port to try to get on a Navy ship to return home as we have to wait until this PM. Thurs Sept 6, 1945 The Col called me into his office and told me he would sure like to see me stay. I stood there. He said it won't be too long and he said I can fly home with him. So I said Col I will stay. He was so happy about it all. Sunday Sept 10 I was to go to Saipan for processing to go home. Now I must stay until the Group goes. Here it is Sept 27, 1945 A Sgt Grimes came over and said I must fly home Sept 28 with the 444 Group plane. I am all excited about it, and tonite I fed the Col and his company their last meal.

sat night we sent a Victory flight over Ramey & Col Kal, they left and I told taken off the now I had to go asked the Gen back on the list tomarrow the 3rd sunday noon 40 planes to return Gee I can't sleep xcited. Well here and still packed to go A.T.C. But it this morning I to try to get on

out our planes for toyko and Gen had Eatin before Kal that I was loading list, that by boat, so Kal to have me put to fly Home of Sept, and now its waiting for our about 4:30 this P.M. or eat I am to it is tue the 4th & waiting we were was Cancelled. So went to the port a navy ship to

return Home, as until this P.M. the Col called me told me he sure stay, so I stood it won't be too you can fly home said Col. I will Happy about it all to go to sipian for Home. now I must Group goes. So here a Sgt Grimers Cone I fly Home Sept 28 so I am all xcited tonight I fed the thier last meal

we have to wait Thur Sept 6, 1945 into his office and would like me to thier and he said long and he said with me. So I stay, he was so Sunday 10, I was prossering to go stay until the it is Sept 27, 1945 over and said I must with 444 cyp plane about it, and Col & his Company

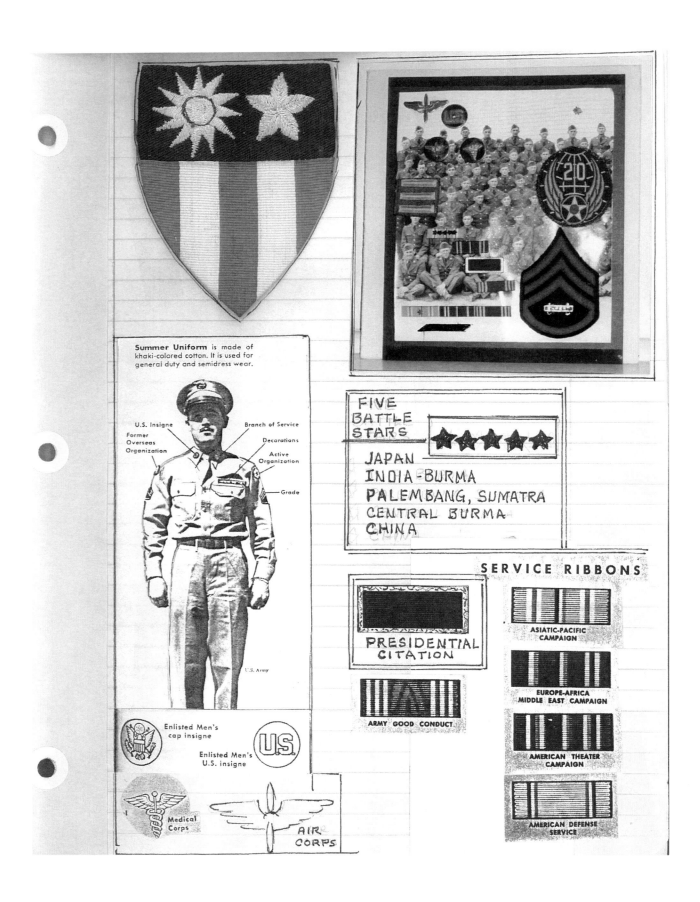

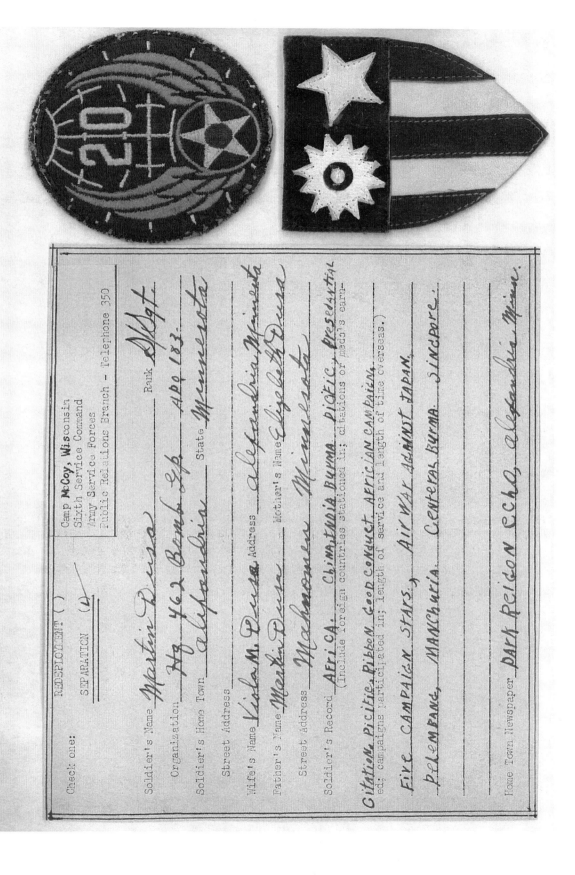

Check one:
REDEPLOYMENT ( )
SEPARATION (✓)

Camp McCoy, Wisconsin
Sixth Service Command
Army Service Forces
Public Relations Branch - Telephone 350

Soldier's Name **Martin Deura** Rank **S/Sgt.**
Organization **Hq 462 Bomb Gp** **APO 183.**
Soldier's Home Town **Alexandria** State **Minnesota**
Street Address
Wife's Name **Viola M. Deura** Address **Alexandria, Minnesota**
Father's Name **Martin Deura** Mother's Name **Elizabeth Deura**
Street Address **Mahnomen, Minnesota**
Soldier's Record **Africa, China,India,Burma. Pacific. African campaign.**
(Include foreign countries stationed in; citations or medal's earned; campaigns participated in; length of service and length of time overseas.)
Citations **Pacific Ribbon. Good Conduct. African Campaign.**
Five Campaign Stars., Airway Against Japan.
Palembang, Manchuria. Central Burma. Singapore.

Home Town Newspaper **Park Region Echo, Alexandria, Minn.**

Bombardment Squadron
462nd Bombardment Group
APO 183, c/o Postmaster
San Francisco, California

CLOTHING AND ADJUSTMENT FORM

28 September 1945

Clothing	Allowance	In Possession of E.M.	Clothing	Allowance	In Possession of E.M.
BELT, Web, Waist	1 ea	1	NECKTIE, Cotton	2 ea	2
CAP, Garrison, Khk	1 ea	1	RAINCOAT, Dism't	1 ea	1
*CAP, Garrison, OD	1 ea	1	SHIRT, Ctn. Khk.	2 ea	2
CAP or HAT, HBT	1 ea	1	*SHIRT, Wool, OD	1 ea	1
*COAT, Wool, Serge	1 ea	1	SHOES, Service	2 pr	2
DRAWERS, Cotton	3 pr	3	SOCKS, Ctn or Wool	4 pr	4
HANDKERCHIEFS	4 ea	4	SUITS, 1 Pc. HBT	1 ea	0
*INSIGNIA, 20th AF	3 ea	3	TROUSERS, Ctn. Khk	2 pr	2
JACKET, Field, OD	1 ea	1	*TROUSERS, Wool, OD	1 pr	1
JACKET, HBT(when not suit, 1 pc)	1 ea	1	TROUSERS, HBT(when not suit 1 pc)	1 pr	1
LACES, Shoe	1 pr	1	UNDERSHIRT, Smr, Sl'les	3 ea	3

Equipment	Allowance	In Possession of E.M.		Allowance	In Possession of E.M.
BAG, Bks. or Duffel	1 ea	1	STRAP, Carrying, Bag	1 ea	1
BAG, Field, OD	1 ea	1	SPOON	1 ea	1
BELT, Pistol	1 ea	1	NECKLACE, Identification, W/Ext.	1 ea	1
BLANKET, Wool, OD	2 ea	0			
CAN, Meat	1 ea	1	TAG, Identification	2 ea	2
CANTEEN	1 ea	1	TOILET, Articles	1 set	1
COVER, Canteen	1 ea	1	TOWEL, Bath	2 ea	2
CUP, Canteen	1 ea	1	MASK, Gas, equipped w/eyeglasses, Gas		
FORK	1 ea	1			
KNIFE	1 ea	1	Mask, M-1 only	1 ea	0

* To be taken if in the hands of troops at present. No stock available at QM Depot for issue.

The items listed hereon constitute all the Government Clothing and Individual Equipment in the possession of **Martin Dusa** (name) **S/Sgt** (rank) **17049855** (serial no.) upon departure from this Command. All other items of clothing and equipment have been withdrawn and returned to stock or otherwise disposed of in accordance with regulations. Adjustment of clothing and equipment is made pursuant to Circular No. 72, WD., 1945.

Signed: *Martin Dusa*   Signed: *H. K. Chatterton*   "Certified Correct"

Martin Dusa 17049855   H. K. CHATTERTON,
Type name and ASN   Type name
S/Sgt   1st Lt., Air Corps,
Grade   Group Supply Officer.

"Certifying Officer"

RESTRICTED

CALIFORNIA
CAMP STONEMAN, PITTSBURG
MATHER FIELD, SACRAMENTO
CAMP McCOY, WISCONSIN

Par 8 SO 129, Hq 58th Bomb Wg (Cont'd)

For Separation Center #33, Camp McCoy, Wisconsin
44th Bomb Sq, 40th Bomb Gp

Sgt (911) Henry J Lipinski 16134590 (90), 746 S. 24th St., Milwaukee, Wisc
Cpl (747) Robert J Nehiba 17050891 (89(, 2722 4th Ave, West, Hibbing, Minn.

45th Bomb Sq, 40th Bomb Gp

Sgt (756) Peter Penasa 16089466 (88), 2473-A N. 22nd St., Milwaukee, Wis.
T Sgt (542) Roy L Franklin 36251390 (90), La Crosse, Wis.
S Sgt (747) George J Singer 16005328 (89), 3456 S. 8th St., Milwaukee, Wis.

676th Bomb Sq, 444th Bomb Gp

Cpl (756) Charles Oakes 37292739 (81) Wawina, Minn.
T Sgt (737) Frank J Pudelko 16021644 (80), Rothschild, Wis.

677th Bomb Sq, 444th Bomb Gp

T Sgt (750) Herman J Otto 16128947 (94), Mendovi, Wis.
S Sgt (750) Harvey C Tredup 36813587 (71), 67__, 28th St., Kenosha, Wis.
S Sgt (747) George E Weber 36290732 (79), 2362 N. 64th St., Wanwatosa, Wis.
S Sgt (2756) Robert G Kanies 16117324 (81), 3714A W. Lisbon Ave., Milwaukee, Wis.
Sgt (747) Joseph D Turner 36227850 (89), RFD #1, Eastman, Wis.

768th Bomb Sq, 462d Bomb Gp

S Sgt (685) Maynard O Pierce 14138717 (92), College Park, Ga.

678th Bomb Sq, 444th Bomb Gp

T Sgt (737) Domenic Cipollone 37021560 (72), Gen. Del., Hibbing, Minn.
M Sgt (750) John J Diedrich 36212297 (92), New Diggings, Wis.
1ST LT (1031) JOHN N MASON 07___ AC (82), Williams, Minn.
1ST LT (1036) JOSEPH _ _____ 0691694 AC (105), 319 Bryant Ave. Wadena, Minn.
1ST LT (1093) FRANCIS W BLANCH 0759396 AC (84), Kasson, Minn

S Sgt (060) Martin Dusa 17049855 (93), Alexandria, Minn.
Sgt (673) Robert L Stinson 37004752 (89), Maple Plain, Minn

768th Bomb Sq, 462d Bomb Gp

Sgt (901) Melvin C Neutz 17047400 (88), North Minneapolis, Minn.

770th Bomb Sq, 462d Bomb Gp

Sgt (747) Clarence A Behnke 36268983 (91), Ft. Atkinson, Wis.
Cpl (345) Robert P Driscoll 37543452 (89), St. Paul, Minn.

792d Bomb Sq, 468th Bomb Gp

Sgt (901) Robert C Michael 34601019 (93), 2714 E. Menlo Blvd., Milwaukee, Wis.
Sgt (611) Harvey L Wallin 17047181 (98), Munger Terrace, Duluth, Minn.
SSgt (1685) John A Stich 16134698 (95), Route 2, Box 122, Hales Corner, Wis.

794th Bomb Sq, 468th Bomb Gp

Sgt (747) John C Bruhn 37094907 (94), 439 E. Sheridan St., Ely, Minn.

35th Air Eng Sq., 25th Air Sv Gp

Cpl (405) Christian F Nielsen 20655779 (91), 5671 N. 34th St., Milwaukee 10, Wis.

323th Signal Co., Wing

T Sgt (766) Luke Frye 36219202 (90), Lona, Wis.

* * *   * * *   * * *

BY COMMAND OF BRIGADIER GENERAL RAMEY:
                                RAMEY

OFFICIAL:

Ross Langley
ROSS LANGLEY
Major, Air Corps
Adjutant

D. O. MONTEITH
Colonel, Air Corps
Chief of Staff

RESTRICTED

RESTRICTED
1st Ind   AGC-7E/ajm

PAE, 1505th AAFBU, ACW, PD-ATC, Mather Field, Sacramento, Calif, 2 Oct 45

TO: Commanding General, Camp Stoneman, Pittsburg, California.

    Personnel listed on attached order with exception of those destined for Camp Beale, Calif, having arrived this PAE from overseas this date IAW attached orders.

    FOR THE COMMANDING OFFICER:

                                      R. G. HOPP
                                      Capt., AC
                                      Asst Adj

WESTERN UNION

CLASS OF SERVICE
This is a full-rate Telegram or Cablegram unless its deferred character is indicated by a suitable symbol above or preceding the address.

A. N. WILLIAMS
PRESIDENT

1204

SYMBOLS
DL = Day Letter
NL = Night Letter
LC = Deferred Cable
NLT = Cable Night Letter
Ship Radiogram

The filing time shown in the date line on telegrams and day letters is STANDARD TIME at point of origin. Time of receipt is STANDARD TIME at point of destination.

11M K 16

CAMP STONEMAN CALIF 822 AM OCT 5 1945

MRS MARTIN DUSA
    ALEXANDRIA MINN

LEAVING TODAY FOR CAMP MCCOY WIS SENT PACKAGE DO NOT OPEN WILL INFORM YOU UPON ARRIVAL.

                MARTIN DUSA 1046 AM

Oct. 2. Telephone Call from Pittsburg, CA
Oct. 5. Telegram
Oct. 6. Ogden, Utah - Telegram
Oct. 7. Denver, Co. Telegram
Oct. 8. Chicago, Ill. phone call
Oct. 9. McCoy, Wis - phone call
Oct. 14. Arrived Home.

MARTIN DUSA JR 17 049 855 STAFF SERGEANT
HEADQUARTERS 462ND BOMB GROUP

Army of the United States

is hereby Honorably Discharged from the military service of the United States of America.
This certificate is awarded as a testimonial of Honest and Faithful Service to this country.

Given at: Separation Center, Camp McCoy Wisconsin

Date: 13 October 1945

Arthur H. Schmitz
Major Sig C

ENLISTED RECORD AND REPORT OF SEPARATION—HONORABLE DISCHARGE

1. LAST NAME – FIRST NAME – MIDDLE INITIAL	2. ARMY SERIAL NO.	3. GRADE	4. ARM OR SERVICE	5. COMPONENT
Dusa Jr., Martin	17 049 855	S/Sgt	AAF	AUS

6. ORGANIZATION	7. DATE OF SEPARATION	8. PLACE OF SEPARATION
HQ 462nd Bomb Gp	13 Oct 45	Separation Center Camp McCoy Wisconsin

9. PERMANENT ADDRESS FOR MAILING PURPOSES	10. DATE OF BIRTH	11. PLACE OF BIRTH
Alexandria, Minn	27 Feb 1915	Chicago, Ill

12. ADDRESS FROM WHICH EMPLOYMENT WILL BE SOUGHT	13. COLOR EYES	14. COLOR HAIR	15. HEIGHT	16. WEIGHT	17. NO. DEPEND.
See 9	Blue	Brn	5-8	162	2

18. RACE	19. MARITAL STATUS	20. U S CITIZEN	21. CIVILIAN OCCUPATION AND NO.
WHITE x	SINGLE x	YES x	Salesman House to House 1-55.10

MILITARY HISTORY

22. DATE OF INDUCTION	23. DATE OF ENLISTMENT	24. DATE OF ENTRY INTO ACTIVE SERVICE	25. PLACE OF ENTRY INTO SERVICE
	4 Mar 42	4 Mar 42	Ft Snelling Minn

SELECTIVE SERVICE DATA	26. REGISTERED YES x	27. LOCAL S.S. BOARD NO.	28. COUNTY AND STATE	29. HOME ADDRESS AT TIME OF ENTRY INTO SERVICE
				See 9

30. MILITARY OCCUPATIONAL SPECIALTY AND NO.	31. MILITARY QUALIFICATION AND DATE
Mess Sergeant (824)	None

32. BATTLES AND CAMPAIGNS
India Burma Air Off Japan China Central Burma

33. DECORATIONS AND CITATIONS
Good Conduct Medal

34. WOUNDS RECEIVED IN ACTION
None

35. LATEST IMMUNIZATION DATES				36. SERVICE OUTSIDE CONTINENTAL U.S. AND RETURN		
SMALLPOX	TYPHOID	TETANUS	OTHER (SPECIFY)	DATE OF DEPARTURE	DESTINATION	DATE OF ARRIVAL
Dec.44	Dec.44	Dec.44	Typhus Dec.44*	23 Jan 44	CBI	20 Mar 44
				25 Feb 45	CPTO	6 Apr 45
				Unknown	USA	2 Oct 45

37. TOTAL LENGTH OF SERVICE						38. HIGHEST GRADE HELD
CONTINENTAL SERVICE			FOREIGN SERVICE			
YEARS	MONTHS	DAYS	YEARS	MONTHS	DAYS	
1	11	3	1	8	10	S/Sgt

39. PRIOR SERVICE
None

40. REASON AND AUTHORITY FOR SEPARATION
Convenience of the Govt RR1-1 (Demobilization) AR 615-365 15 Dec 44

41. SERVICE SCHOOLS ATTENDED	42. EDUCATION (YEARS)		
	Grammar	High School	College
None	8	0	0

PAY DATA

43. LONGEVITY FOR PAY PURPOSES			44. MUSTERING OUT PAY		45. Soldier Deposits	46. TRAVEL PAY	47. TOTAL AMOUNT. NAME OF DISBURSING OFFICER
YEARS	MONTHS	DAYS	TOTAL	THIS PAYMENT			
3	7	11	300	100	600.00	20.05	799.67 H L Oldenburg Maj FD

INSURANCE NOTICE

IMPORTANT: If premium is not paid when due or within thirty-one days thereafter, insurance will lapse. Make checks or money orders payable to the Treasurer of the U. S. and forward to Collections Subdivision, Veterans Administration, Washington 25, D. C.

48. KIND OF INSURANCE			49. HOW PAID		50. Effective Date of Allotment Discontinuance	51. Date of Next Premium Due (One Month After 50)	52. Premium Due Each Month	53. INTENTION OF VETERAN TO		
Nat. Serv. x	U.S. Govt.	None	Allotment x	Direct to V.A.	30 Sep 45	31 Oct 45	6.90	Continue	Continue Only	Discontinue x

54. RIGHT THUMB PRINT ((()))

55. REMARKS:
Asiatic Pacific Theater Service Medal
Three Overseas Service Bars No Time Lost Under AW 107
Lapel Button Issued ASR Score 93 (2 Sep 45)
*Cholera Dec 44
Yellow Fever Mar 42

56. SIGNATURE OF PERSON BEING SEPARATED	57. PERSONNEL OFFICER
Martin Dusa	Marie H. Ehler 1st Lt WAC Assistant Adjutant

Filed for Record the 12th day of April A.D. 1946 at 3 o'clock P.M.

Aldrich Ostlund

Reunited with family at Alexandria, Minnesota October 15, 1945

Honor Roll located at Douglas County Court House Alexandria, MN.
Maryann with pointer in hand.

ARMY AIR FORCES
Certificate of Appreciation
FOR WAR SERVICE

TO

Martin Dusa, Jr.

I CANNOT meet you personally to thank you for a job well done; nor can I hope to put in written words the great hope I have for your success in future life.

Together we built the striking force that swept the Luftwaffe from the skies and broke the German power to resist. The total might of that striking force was then unleashed upon the Japanese. Although you no longer play an active military part, the contribution you made to the Air Forces was essential in making us the greatest team in the world.

The ties that bound us under stress of combat must not be broken in peacetime. Together we share the responsibility for guarding our country in the air. We who stay will never forget the part you have played while in uniform. We know you will continue to play a comparable role as a civilian. As our ways part, let me wish you God speed and the best of luck on your road in life. Our gratitude and respect go with you.

H. H. Arnold
COMMANDING GENERAL
ARMY AIR FORCES

THIS IS TO CERTIFY THAT

Martin Dusa, Jr.   S/Sgt   17649855
NAME   GRADE   SERIAL NO.

RATING   ORGANIZATION

SERVED HONORABLY AND WELL IN THE UNITED STATES ARMY AIR FORCES IN WORLD WAR II.

H. H. Arnold
COMMANDING GENERAL
ARMY AIR FORCES

General Arnold has directed that I write to inform you that even though you no longer wear the Air Forces uniform, we of the Air Forces consider you one of us.

The tremendous accomplishment of the Air Forces was only made possible by contributions such as you made.

B-29 - HOODLUM HOUSE II

PAINTINGS
BY
FRED B. MAAR
OF
INDIANAPOLIS, IN
HELLBIRDS
HEADQUARTERS
PHOTOGRAPHER
INDIA
AND
TINIAN

ARTIST USED CHALK AND WATER COLOR.

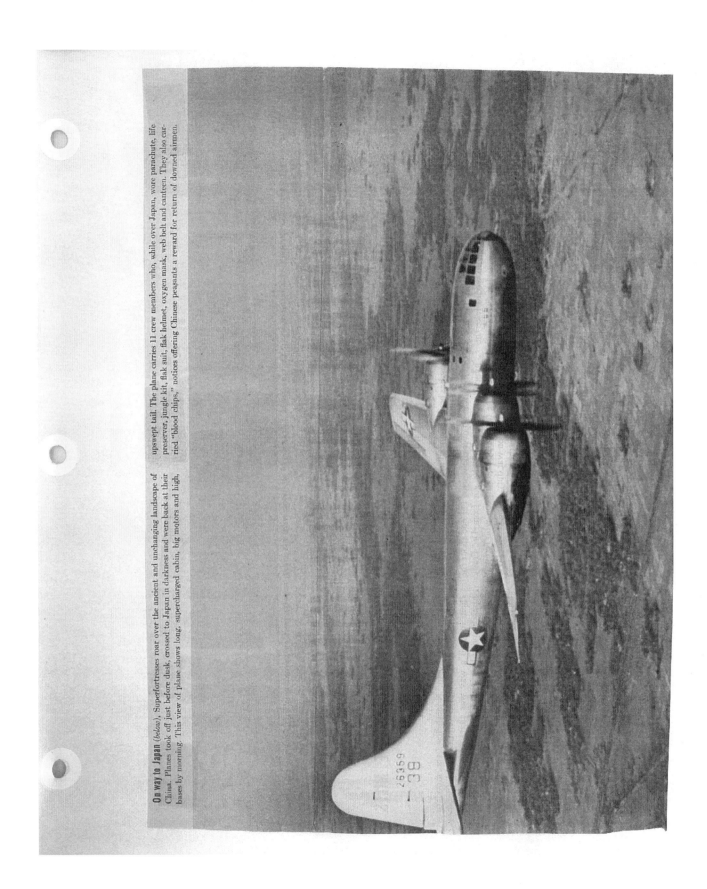

On way to Japan (*below*), Superfortresses roar over the ancient and unchanging landscape of China. Planes took off just before dusk, crossed to Japan in darkness and were back at their bases by morning. This view of plane shows long, supercharged cabin, big motors and high, upswept tail. The plane carries 11 crew members who, while over Japan, wore parachute, life preserver, jungle kit, flak suit, flak helmet, oxygen mask, web belt and canteen. They also carried "blood chips," notices offering Chinese peasants a reward for return of downed airmen.

— CBI IQ —

How many different "Blood Chits" were used in CBI?

Old Kachin Ranger Jim Fletcher knows of five Blood Chits, but believes there were many more. Blood Chits were first used by aviators in the China-Burma-India theater. They included one or more flags and a message in one or more languages asking the native population to assist the man who wore the Blood Chit. Jim sends along photos of four of the chits in his personal collection. They are reproduced below.

A Chinese flag with Chinese writing may have been the first Blood Chit worn by members of the A.V.G. "Flying Tigers," Jim believes. Note that this early Blood Chit does not include an American Flag.

This particular Blood Chit was hand-painted on leather by Chinese workmen. It includes American and Chinese flags and the CBI emblem. The message is in Chinese. Jim reports that this Blood Chit was worn by ground forces. None of the Blood Chits printed here are "Government issue."

An American flag and a message in several languages were the features of this Blood Chit. Jim believes it, too, was worn by some ground troops.

RAF airmen used the Blood Chit above, featuring the WW2 Burma flag with its royal peacock. The message is in Burmese.

The fifth Blood Chit, of course, is the best-known of all. It (not pictured here) included the American and Chinese flags and a message in Chinese or Chinese and English asking anyone who read the message to provide assistance to the wearer.

ERNIE PYLE
The Soldier's Correspondent

Editor's Note: April 1992 marks the 47th anniversary of the death of correspondent Ernie Pyle. Ernie served in many areas of WW II conflict. Although there is no record of Ernie serving in the CBI, many of us knew of his reports that appeared in newspapers and magazines the world over.

Pulitzer Prize winning columnist Ernie Pyle was America's best-known World War II correspondent. Unlike other war correspondents, Pyle Ignored the Generals, politicians, and grand strategies – concentrating instead on the common soldier and his often boring, dirty, frightening, and lonely world. He was a foxhole journalist who lived "up front" with "the boys" and provided the people back home with their only consistently reliable account of what was happening inside the head, heart, belly, and wet shoes of their brothers, husbands, and sons. Ernie's work earned him respect and admiration of both the little guy in the fox hole, his family, and their nation. They all realized Pyle's honest chronicling of common reactions to horrendous events provided some of the truest pictures of the war.

By the time Pyle was killed by a sniper's bullet in 1945, his name was a household word, and he was considered a national hero. President Truman insisted on personally announcing the news of Pyle's death to the nation saying, "No man in this war has so well told the story of the American fighting man as American fighting men wanted it told. He deserves the gratitude of all his countrymen." Fellow Pulitzer Prize winner, Bill Mauldin, put it this way, "The only difference between Ernie's death and the death of any other good guy is that the other guy is mourned by his company. Ernie is mourned by the Army."

After the United States was drawn into the war, Ernie, who was 41 years old by then, tried to enlist but was rejected by the military; so he went to war as a civilian correspondent.

Ernie was killed on Ie Shima, April 18, 1945.

Unlike most correspondents, Ernie never offered any opinions about who was winning or losing the war. He just told little stories about the men fighting it. He drew vignettes with two fingers on his typewriter keys that told more about the victories and defeats of World War II than all the official communiques ever issued.

Ernie Pyle, the Soldier's Corre-
ERNIE PYLE

ERNIE ON PATROL AT OKINAWA. Columnist Ernie Pyle (third from left) trudges along with First Division Marines on patrol in the interior of

MARTIN DUSA
Letter to Son Lee

September 14, 1945

Dearest Son,

Well my boy it will be hard for you to understand this letter, as through no fault of yours or mine we haven't had the pleasure of meeting. But your mother has told me a great deal about you almost every day since you were born. I saw many pictures of you.

Yes, Lee Mother and you have done a great deal for your Daddy while I was in the Army fighting a hard war. First in Africa, then in India, then the Pacific. Yes, I realize its been hard for Mother and you to struggle for so long alone.

But now the war is over and I shall soon join you, and I think we can, and will, all be happier. So son I send you the Best Wishes on your birthday and please mind Mother. And please have faith and respect.

Yours lovingly,
Dad

Sept, 14, 1945

Dearest Son

Well my Boy it will be hard for you to understand this letter, as through no fault of yours or mine we havent had the pleasure of meeting. but your Mother has told me a great deal about you. almost every day since you were born. and I saw many pictures of you. yes Lee Mother and you have done a great deal for your daddy while I was in the army fighting a hard war first in africa then India then the pacific. yes I relize its been hard for Mother and you, to struggle for so long alone. But now the war is over and I soon shall join you, and I think we can, and will all be happier. So Son I send you the Best Wishes on your Birthday, and please mind Mother. So please Have Faith & respect.

Yours Lovelingly
Dad.

MARTIN AND VI -
Life Together After the War

I was born in 1943, halfway through World War II. My Dad greeted me when he returned from service in 1945 when I was two, my first real interaction with my Dad. Reunited with his wife of four years, my Mom, Vi, they began their life together in Alexandria, Minnesota. Dad went back to work for Gambles, the company he left when he enlisted four years earlier. Mom, Dad and I lived with Mom's relatives in Alex for a couple of years. Then Dad agreed to partner with Gust Smith in the formation of a new business located in Henning, Minnesota, a small town about forty miles from Alex. Dad and Gust located an old building on Main Street in Henning to set up shop. Mom, Dad and I lived in a small rental house near the railroad tracks in Green's Addition in northeast Henning. Dad and Mom acquired a building lot in west Henning in the Thompson neighborhood and started construction of their home. Mom drew the plans.

I remember vividly, even though I was four at the time, the way in which the hole for the basement was excavated. There were no bull dozers, backhoes or mechanized equipment of any kind. In fact, excavators and backhoes did not appear in the US until the late 1950's or early sixties. Picture a narrow gravel road going out into the middle of a flat alfalfa field. A building lot, designated by markers 60 foot by 200 feet in size would become this young families' new home. A team of two large horses with heavy leather harnesses were brought in to dig the hole for the basement. Their harness was attached to a Mormon board, a sled like tool with two handles for the operator to manage and attached to the harness by two strong chains. The steel blade of the sled was angled to dig into the soil as the horses moved forward. Two inches of soil were moved to the edge of the lot and dumped by the operator flipping the Mormon board over. The horses were then instructed to back up to the beginning point, with the operator dragging the sled by hand, stopped, and then the operator would lean against the handles of the Mormon board to dig another two inches on the next pass. The operator directed the horses to pull pass after pass and then move over for the next strip. Day after day the hole got deeper until an eight-foot depth was achieved indicating the place where the basement of the house would be located. The team of two horses would climb an ever-higher pile of excavated dirt on the edge of the site, then back down that pile for the next pass. I was amazed to watch this process and will never forget this laborious and time-consuming approach for excavation.

Mom and Dad were building a brand-new home, starting a new business with a new business partner in a town they had not even visited previously. They had one young child (me) and they were very relieved that the war was over. During the four years of the war, they had no idea how things were going to turn out. Reports from the front were grim with both sides making claims of small victories and defeats of the enemy. The country was fighting for its very existence. Hitler had conquered much of Europe, Japan had control of much of the Pacific and the US was losing thousands of soldiers in the war. Finally, in 1945 the course of the war ended rapidly with the Japanese surrender. The people of the US were elated and could breathe more comfortably as they started to focus on returning to life as they had known it before the war. Soldiers came home. My Dad came home. The veterans carried with them the horror that they experienced during the war and now were relieved that was behind them. They embraced the tremendous opportunity to turn their energies to the future. They viewed their future as limited only by their hard work, their application of their skills and their complete appreciation that their home country, now free of potential foreign intervention, could be the launching pad for their family's joyous future. Mom and Dad's attitude was unabashedly optimistic for their own futures and the futures of their kids. They made that clear to me over and over in conversation and by the way they led their lives. It showed. In our small town there were many returning soldiers, each with the same horrific experience of the war, each with the relief that it was all over, and each facing the future with young families that was very optimistic. This was a group of men which were builders, operating under a belief that tomorrow will be better than yesterday. They believed their kids will be more successful and live a better quality of life than they had. And based on several observations I don't think that the veterans in our little town were much different than thousands of returning soldiers all over the US in the late forties. This was the prevailing attitude across America at the time.

I was born into this environment, and it influenced my growing up years until I left home in my late teens. This atmosphere created by Mom and Dad was a significant contributor to the attitudes and points of view I carry with me today. The folks in our town placed a huge importance on education stressing good grades and assuming most of us would go on to college (even if our parents did not). Most residents felt church attendance was necessary as there were eleven churches in our town and if a person did not show up on a given Sunday they would get a phone call wondering if something was wrong. Transparency in the community was complete as everyone knew everyone else and if a person did a deed that was questionable, they would be talked about. It was important not to be "talked about". It was important to find an area to excel and to establish a reputation that indicted that you were applying your skills in a productive manner in some pursuit. What others thought of you was very important and it was critical those thoughts people held about you were positive in nature. It was important to prepare for the future as one could realistically achieve a high quality of life, based on their own hard work and success in higher education. The formula for success was clearly understood.

The war experience permeated throughout the community although there was a noticeable difference between the local farmers, who had stayed on the farms to raise food for the population during the war, and the actual soldiers who had worn the uniform. The veterans set up businesses in town upon returning after the war. And, based upon their common experience brought them closer together, they worked as a community to build a new life. Howard Trana became the postmaster, Dan Soutor started the Federated store, Dad ran Home and Farm Supply along with his partner, Dick Cordes ran the John Deere store, Frank Stewart owned FR Stewart Plumbing and Heating, Knute Nord became the railroad agent, Ken Brutlag started the grocery store, Harold Pikal started Harold's Meats and on and on. These veterans built a VFW (Veterans of Forgein Wars) club house on the hill by the water tower where they would meet. Their wives, as members of the Auxiliary, would meet there as well. The veterans saved their uniforms from their service days and wore them as they marched in local parades carrying the flag as the color guard. They were proud and patriotic and very thankful.

Mom kept her Auxiliary uniform next to Dad's military uniforms in the attic closet in our home.

Memorial Day was a well-attended event in our town and taken very seriously. The job of selling the red handmade poppies downtown was performed by the Auxiliary members including Mom. Everyone in town ended up wearing a red poppy on their collars or shirts. The Memorial Day ceremony in the auditorium at the high school was always packed with local folks. This was the time of the year when lilacs were in full bloom and large bouquets of them populated the venue. Mom was on the agenda one year, reading the poem "In Flanders Fields" among other participants including local pastors and the school marching band. After the parade through town the gathering at the cemetery was particularly impressive. The color guard was supplemented with a rifle squad; a bugle player was hidden behind some bushes. After a series of commands from the military leader, the bugle player played "TAPS" from his hidden position, with the notes piercing the gathered crowd with their solemnness. Then the guns were raised and fired three times in a loud jarring salute. The smoke from the guns drifted through the crowd, standing scattered among the white headstones. The commander then demanded a moment of silence from the crowd. No one attending could ever forget this touching remembrance of fallen soldiers.

These veterans took turns serving on the city council, started a Rod and Gun Club, served as Boy Scout Scoutmasters, manned a volunteer fire department, served on the school board, created a summer time three-day Harvest Festival, served fried fish to the whole community at Fireman's Park on a certain Sunday in the spring, met for coffee at 9am every work day at Bondy's Café, went to church every Sunday and raised their kids. The population of the town grew and the population of the school grew. They also started a Civil Defense chapter and a lookout tower.

These veterans had seen the shocking result of the use of atomic weapons which killed thousands and ended the war. They quickly agreed to help in any way possible to avert any further wars and therefore assembled a local group to assist in Civil Defense, a nationwide program in the late forties and early fifties. They built a glass enclosed watch tower on top of the fire station located in the middle of town. They also installed an air raid siren which could be heard for miles during its monthly testing (noon on the first Friday of every month). They took turns sitting in that glass lookout tower from dawn to dusk every day, and using field glasses, scanned the skies for enemy airplanes. Note: our town, near to the northern border of the US, was in an ideal place to spot aircraft coming from Russia over the north pole route. The Cold War was real for us. For several years from ages 5 through 12 I remember visiting that tower. I also remember drills at school diving under our desks, listening to instructions to close our eyes as the flash of the bomb would hurt our vision.

There were many items from the war around our home with which we used growing up. We had several army green pure wool blankets on our beds; Dad had an 8MM German Mauser rifle he used for hunting deer which he brought home from the war. Mom had scrapbooks and boxes of war time documents, newspaper clippings and letters from/to Dad stored in many cardboard boxes in our basement. These later became the basis for this wonderful WWII diary Mom authored. We had an army pup tent we used often to "play" army games in our neighborhood. It had two wooden support poles, each composed of three segments, and several stakes for the corners, but no floor. For our play we also used Dad's white metal Civil Defense helmet as a part of our "uniform". We also used several army green stocking caps for both play and for wintertime warmth. A very unique item was a pair of flight pants used by airmen to keep warm in unheated airplanes during the war. I used these pants frequently when I got big enough when it was really cold outside. They were constructed of dark brown leather and lined with pure white wool fleece about two inches thick and held up with suspenders. They were extremely warm but difficult to walk in so I used them primarily for ice fishing. And Dad brought home many mementos: a hookah pipe from India, a carved black onyx panther, several artillery shells, a ceramic parrot, a silk map of Indonesia used by pilots, and lots of b/w photos taken in the places where he was stationed in his round the world four-year trip. Our family values these treasures today.

The US government during WWII requested all families at home plant vegetable gardens in their yards with an objective of creating an additional food supply for the nation. Called Victory

Gardens, it was a patriotic thing to do and virtually every homeowner in our town had one. We had a large one with every kind of vegetable planted in very straight rows. Dad took pride in keeping the weeds out. As kids we were dispatched to a lot of garden duty by our parents. And it paid off with volumes of fresh veggies during the summer and enough for significant canning come fall.

The war had permeated Mom and Dad's life, their habits, and attitudes to their cores. We four kids felt that influence and carry much of that with us today, albeit somewhat diminished, now after 80 years.

Martin and Vi, after starting married life under the cloud of war, remained happily married until Martin's passing in 1976 due to health issues. Our mom passed in 2013. We four kids have had the most wonderful upbringing that anyone could imagine, due to the strong character of each of our parents. We thank them and honor them for who they were. Lee Dusa

Lee

ADDENDUM

The China, Burma, India (CBI) Campaign –
PRIARDOBA AIRFIELD

During World War II, the airfield hosted the United States Army Air Force 462nd Bombardment Group prior to its deployment to the Mariana Islands.

Piardoba was originally designed for Consolidated B-24 Liberator use. In 1943 it was designated as a Boeing B-29 Superfortress base for the planned deployment of the United States Army Air Forces XX Bomber Command to India. Advance Army Air Forces echelons arrived in India in December 1943 to organize the upgrading of the airfield and thousands of Indians labored to upgrade the facility for Superfortress operations. It was one of four B-29 bases established by the Americans in India. Piardoba was designated to be the home of the 462nd Bombardment Group, with initially four B-29 Squadrons 768th, 769th, 770th and 771st). Support elements of the group included the 9th, 10th, 11th and 12th Bomb Maintenance Squadrons; the 13th Photo Lab, and the 86th Air Service Group. The 462nd arrived at the base on 7 April 1944 after completing B-29 transition training at Walker AAF, Kansas. The deployment to India took almost three weeks, consisting of traveling to Morrision Field, Florida, then south though the Caribbean to Natal, Brazil. From Brazil the South Atlantic was crossed arriving in West Africa and re-assembling at Marrakesh, Morocco. The group then flew north and west from Morocco through Algeria and Egypt, before arriving at Karachi. By the time the group arrived at Piardoba, the month-long trip had taken its toll on the aircraft and personnel.

The 462nd was part of the Operation Matterhorn project of XX Bomber Command, the bombing of the Japanese Home Islands. In order to reach Japan, the B-29s of the group needed to stage operations from Kuinglai (Linqiong) Airfield (A-4), a forward base just to the southwest of Chendu in south-central China. However, in order to stage missions and operate from Kuinglai, the group need to transport supplies of fuel, bombs, and spares needed 1,200 miles to the airfield. Six round trips were necessary to deliver enough fuel for one airplane to mount a combat mission from China – an impractical logistics concept for an aerial campaign. Almost immediately upon arrival in India, engine fires caused the grounding of all of the groups B-29s. The cause was that the B-29's R-3350 engine had not been designed to operate at ground temperatures higher than 115 degrees F, which were typically exceeded in India. Modifications had also to be made to the aircraft and after these modifications, B-29 flights to India were resumed.

The first combat mission by the group took place on June 5, 1944 when squadrons of the 462nd took off from India to attack the Makasan railroad yards at Bangkok, Thailand. This involved a 2261-mile round trip, the longest bombing mission yet attempted during the war. On June 15 the group participated in the first American Air Force attack on the Japanese Home Islands since the Doolittle raid in 1942. Operating from bases in India, and at times staging through fields in India and China, the group struck transportation centers, naval installations, iron works, aircraft plants, and other targets in Japan, Thailand, Burma, China, Formosa, and Indonesia. From a staging base in Ceylon, the 462nd mined the Moesi River on Sumatra in August 1944. Received a Distinguished Unit Citation for a daylight attack on iron and steel works at Yawata, Japan, in August 1944. The 462nd evacuated staging fields in China in January 1945 due to the Japanese offensive in South China which threatened the forward staging bases, but continued operations from India, bombing targets in Thailand and mining waters around Singapore. However, by late 1944 it was becoming apparent that B-29 operations against Japan staged out of the bases in Chengtu were far too expensive in men and materials and would have to be stopped. In December 1944, the Joint Chiefs of Staff made the decision that Operation Matterhorn would be phased out, and the B-29s would be moved to newly-captured bases in the Marianas in the central Pacific. On 26 February 1945, the 462nd Bombardment Group flew south to Ceylon, then southeast across the Indian Ocean to Perth in Western Australia. Flying north through New Guinea, it reached its new home at West Field, Tinian, in the Mariana Islands on 4 April where it and its parent 58th Bombardment Wing came under the command of the new XXI Bomber Command. With the departure of the B-29s to the Marianas, Piardoba Airfield was turned over to the Tenth Air Force. The 33rd Fighter Group moved to the airfield on 5 May 1945 after being withdrawn from Combat. The group left its P-38s and P-47s at the airfield for disposal, with the personnel returning to the United States. The unit was inactivated in mid-November.

ABOUT THE HELLBIRDS

The Japanese called the B-29s that began bombing their homeland in June 1944 the "birds from hell". The 462nd Bomb Group adopted the name "Hellbirds" on their recommendation. This site is dedicated to those brave men who served as Hellbirds.

No Japanese territory was outside the reach of the Hellbirds. From their bases in Piradoba, West Bengal, India, Kiunglai, Chengdu, China, and West Field, Tinian, the Hellbirds helped bring Japan to her knees with 15 months of incessant and increasingly accurate bombings.

The Hellbirds flew the first B-29 overseas, flying from the US to England, Marrakech, Cairo, Karachi, and Kharagpur in early 1944.

The Hellbirds were the first to fly the B-29 over the hump to Kiunglai, Chengdu, China, and back to India.

The Hellbirds flew many missions with the other three groups from the 58th Bomb Wing. With these Groups, the Hellbirds were also first to:

- Introduce the advanced B-29 into battle for the first time – Bangkok – 5 June 1944

- Bomb mainland Japan, the first such mission since Jimmy Doolittle did it on 18 April 1942, at Yawata on 15 June 1944.

The Hellbirds trained in western Kansas, near the towns of Hays, Victoria and Walker. After the long winter of 1943-44, the Hellbird crews took their new B-29s to their main base at Piaradoba, many via the Modification Centers scattered throughout the US. The remaining men went by boat.

The Hellbirds flew missions all throughout Asia, including mainland Japan. Bombing Japan required staging raids from Kiunglai, and exposed the Hellbird crews to the dangers of flying the Hump.

After 11 months in Asia, the 58th Bomb Wing moved their operations to Tinian Island in the Marianas, where in 4 months the Hellbirds joined the rest of the 20th Air Force in bringing down the Japanese, without the need for a costly invasion.

The Hellbirds won three Distinguished Unit Citations during WWII…for missions to Yawata, Tokyo/Yokohama and Takarazuka.

BOEING B-29 SUPERFORTRESS

Boeing submitted the proposal for the B-29 long-range heavy bomber to the Army in 1940, before the United States entered World War II. One of the most technologically advanced airplanes of World War II, the B-29 had many new features, including guns that could be fired by remote control. Two crew areas, fore and aft, were pressurized and connected by a long tube over the bomb bays, allowing crew members to crawl between them. The tail gunner had a separate pressurized area that could only be entered or left at altitudes that did not require pressurization. The B-29 was also the world's heaviest production plane because of increases in range, bomb load and defensive requirements.

The B-29 used the high-speed Boeing 117 airfoil, and its larger Fowler flaps added to the wing area as they increased lift. Modifications led to the B-29D, upgraded to the B-50, and the RB-29 photoreconnaissance aircraft. The Soviet-built copy of the B-29 was called the Tupolev Tu-4.

The earliest B-29s were built before testing was finished, so the Army established modification centers where last-minute changes could be made without slowing expanding assembly lines.

Boeing built a total of 2,766 B-29s at plants in Wichita, Kan., (previously the Stearman Aircraft Co., merged with Boeing in 1934) and in Renton, Wash. The Bell Aircraft Co. built 668 of the giant bombers in Georgia, and the Glenn L. Martin Co. built 536 in Nebraska. Production ended in 1946.

B-29s were primarily used in the Pacific theater during World War II. As many as 1,000 Superfortresses at a time bombed Tokyo, destroying large parts of the city. Finally, on Aug. 6, 1945, the B-29 *Enola Gay* dropped the world›s first atomic bomb on Hiroshima, Japan. Three days later a second B-29, *Bockscar,* dropped another atomic bomb on Nagasaki. Shortly thereafter, Japan surrendered.

After the war, B-29s were adapted for several functions, including in-flight refueling, antisubmarine patrol, weather reconnaissance and rescue duty. The B-29 saw military service again in Korea between 1950 and 1953, battling new adversaries: jet fighters and electronic weapons. The last B-29 in squadron use retired from service in September 1960.

| The Hellbirds
462nd Bomb Group (VH) – From the CBI to the Marianas	

History of the 462nd Bombardment Group

Source: **AIR FORCE COMBAT UNITS OF WORLD WAR I1**
Edited by Maurer Maurer

Office of Air Force History
Washington, D.C.
1983

462nd BOMBARDMENT GROUP

Constituted as 462nd Bombardment Group (Heavy) on 19 May 1943. Activated on 1 Jul 1943. Redesignated 462nd Bombardment Group (Very Heavy) in Nov 1943. Prepared for combat with B-29's. Moved to the CBI theater, via Africa, Mar-Jun 1944. Assigned to Twentieth AF in Jun 1944. Transported supplies over the Hump to staging fields in China before entering combat with an attack on railroad shops at Bangkok, Thailand, on 5 Jun 1944. On 15 Jun 1944 took part in the first AAF strike on the Japanese home islands since the Doolittle raid in 1942. Operating from India and China, bombed transportation centers, naval installations, iron works, aircraft plants, and other targets in Japan, Thailand, Burma, China, Formosa, and Indonesia. From a staging base in Ceylon, mined the Moesi River on Sumatra in Aug 1944. Received a DUC for a daylight attack on iron and steel works at Yawata, Japan, in Aug 1944.

Moved to Tinian in the spring of 1945 for further operations against targets in Japan. Participated in mining operations, bombardment of strategic targets, and incendiary raids on urban areas. Bombed industrial areas in Tokyo and Yokohama in May 1945, being awarded a DUC for the action. Received another DUC for a daylight attack on an aircraft plant at Takarazuka on 24 Jul 1945. Returned to the US late in 1945. Assigned to Strategic Air Command on 21 Mar 1946. Inactivated on 31 Mar 1946.

Squadrons. 345th: 1945-1946. 768th: 1943-1946. 769th: 1943-1946. 770th: 1943-1946. 771st: 1943-1944.

Stations. Smoky Hill AAFld, Kan, 1 Jul 1943; Walker AAFld, Kan, 28 Jul 1943-12 Mar 1944; Piardoba, India, 7 Apr 1944-26 Feb 1945; West Field, Tinian, 4 Apr-5 Nov 1945; MacDill Field, Fla, Nov 1945-31 Mar 1946.

Commanders. Unkn, 1 Jul-5 Aug 1943; Col Alan D Clark, 5 Aug 1943; Col Richard H Carmichael, 26 Aug 1943; Col Alfred F Kalberer, 20 Aug 1944-unkn.

Campaigns. American Theater; India-Burma; Air Offensive, Japan; China Defensive; Western Pacific; Central Burma.

Decorations. Distinguished Unit Citations: Yawata, Japan, 20 Aug 1944; Tokyo and Yokohama, Japan, 23, 25, and 29 May 1945; Takarazuka, Japan, 24 Jul 1945.

Insigne. None.

MAJOR GENERAL ALFRED F. KALBERER

About 22,000 flying hours separate the "yesterday" when 17 year old Alfred F. Kalberer became a pilot and the "today" which finds him a major general and chief of staff, Allied Air Forces, Southern Europe, Naples, Italy.

World War II mililary aviation histories report such facts as the organization and leadership (by Colonel Kalberer) of a flight of eight heavy bombers against the Italian fleet – with such heavy enemy losses inflicted that its surrender was the inevitable result. Kalberar led his group on the last heavy bombardment of the Japanese home islands on the day they surrendered. By that time he had flown 46 combat missions as a B-24 and B-29 pilot in the middle and Far East.

"I learn something new every time I make a flight," the general tells associates. The general is as ardent an athlete as a pilot. For midday relaxation he spends most lunchtimes on the badminton court, and was a member of the doubles championship team of the Strategic Air Command.

Alfred F. Kalberer was born at Lafayette, Ind., in 1907. He had already learned to fly when he received an appointment as an air cadet in 1927. Commissioned a reserve second lieutenant the following year at Kelly Field, Texas, he was assigned to the 1st Pursuit Group, Selfridge Field, Mich.

In 1929 he resigned from active duty to make a 50,000 mile advertising tour of the United States, Mexico and Cuba for the General Tire and Rubber Co. He then became an airmail pilot for the National Air Transport. While with NAT – later known as Eastern Division, United Airlines – he flew 8,700 accident-free hours.

When not flying, he wrote nationally published articles and stories, in addition to radio scripts and screenplays. Today, he has less time for writing. However, when time permits, he writes occasional articles and is working on a book about William the Conqueror.

He resigned from United Air Lines in the mid thirties and joined the Royal Dutch Air Lines (KLM). First he lived in Amsterdam, making flights to all of Europe's capitals and to the Dutch East Indies. With the outbreak of the war in Italy, he moved to Bandoeing, Java, and flew in the Far East. Early in the fall of 1941, a Japanese airline pilot told Kalberar that Japan would be at war with the United States before Christmas. He promptly returned to the States on a three-month leave from KLM.

Timing was right. He arrived in Washington Dec. 7, 1941 and returned to active duty as a first lieutenant Dec. 10 assigned to the Army Air Corps' Ferry Command. Shortly thereafter, he was transferred to the Halpro Task Force; which was slated to attack Japan from China with B-24s. From Egypt the bomber force made the first raid on the Ploesti oil field in June 1942 with 13 B-24s. Ploesti was not attacked again until August 1943.

Because of losses, the task force did not go to China, but remained in Egypt to become the nucleus of the Ninth Bomber Command. Kalberer, by this time a major, was named operations officer for the newly formed command. In late June of 1943, he returned to the United States as a lieutenant colonel to enter the B-29 program.

Less than a year later, he was in India as deputy commander of the B-29 equipped 462nd Bomb Group. When its commander was shot down in August 1944, Kalberer assumed command of the group and was promoted to full colonel. His group moved to Tinian in the Marianas in April 1945. It returned to the United States in October, a month after the Japanese surrendered.

In April 1946 Colonel Kalberer was sent to Kwajalein as intelligence officer for Task Group 1.5, the Air Force unit that participated in the Bikini A-bomb tests. He returned to the United States in the fall of 1946 for assignment to Headquarters Eighth Air Force at Forth Worth, Texas, and served as chief of intelligence with the Eighth from September 1946 to December 1947.

While commander of the 55th Reconnaissance Group (later wing) from late 1947 to October 1948, he again participated in atomic tests. He was in charge of photography during the Sandstone

Atomic Weapons Test at Eniwetok Atoll. Colonel Kalberer twice commanded the 55th – first at MacDill Field, Fla., then moved it to Topeka, Kan., in July 1948, where it was deactivated. After a three-year tour at Headquarters SAC as director of public relations and special assistant to the commander in chief – at that time, General Curtis E. LeMay – he again took command of the 55th now reactivated as a medium strategic reconnaissance wing based at Ramey Air Force Base, Puerto Rico. The 55th SRW seemed unable to remain away from Kansas and was again sent to Topeka in October, 1952, while Colonel Kalberer activated and took command of the 72nd SRW (Heavy), a B-36 unit which was built up at Ramey.

Command of the 14th Air Division at Travis Air Force Base, Calif, came next for General Kalberer in August 1955. He had been promoted to one-star rank in December 1952 while at Ramey. He was appointed deputy commander, 15th Air Force and promoted to major general in August 1957.

On July 14, 1959, General Kalberer became vice commander, Headquarters Continental Air Command, Mitchel Air Force Base, N.Y. Two years later, in July 1961, he became chief of staff, Allied Air Forces Southern Europe, Naples, Italy.